Tribal Church

Ministering to the Missing Generation

Carol Howard Merritt

Martha,

Peace to you,

Carol Howard Merritt

THE
ALBAN
INSTITUTE

Herndon, Virginia
www.alban.org

The Alban Institute
2121 Cooperative Way, Suite 100
Herndon, VA 20171

Cover design by Spark Design, LLC

Library of Congress Cataloging-in-Publication Data

Merritt, Carol Howard.
   Tribal church : ministering to the missing generation / Carol Howard
Merritt.
      p. cm.
   Includes bibliographical references.
   ISBN 978-1-56699-347-0 (alk. paper)
   1. Church work with youth. 2. Church work with young adults.
3. Intergenerational relations--Religious aspects--Christianity. I. Title.

   BV4447.M465 2007
   259'.25--dc22

                        2007027473

10   09   08   UG   5   4   3   2

Contents

Contents

Foreword

A couple of years ago, while keynoting an event on the future of the church, I heard a presentation about a population in North America which many people persist in calling "Generation X." The more fervently the speaker argued, the less convinced I became of his analysis. The conversations in small groups, following his presentation, only added to my growing suspicion and unease.

One person after another echoed the speaker's sentiments that the generations following the Baby Boomers represent some sort of backsliding from the "high ideals" and "social activism" of their parents and grandparents. One person after another agreed that these newer generations are represented by slackers, lacking in professional ambition but doubly endowed with a sense of entitlement. If my compatriots were to be believed, the average young person possesses the attention span of a gerbil, the social consciousness of a hermit crab, and the dependency of an intestinal parasite.

The portrait painted of these young people does not square with the college and graduate students I have met and the seminarians I have taught in recent years, or, for that matter, with my own children, both of whom fall smack in the middle of "Generation X." Perhaps it is simply in the nature of things for every generation to believe that it faced and overcame valiantly the great challenges presented by its era, while defaming the character and efforts of those who follow. But, natural or not, this is an impulse we should resist if, that is, we want to understand and respond appropriately to the needs of this generation.

I have been as disturbed by the anxiety rippling through the various conversations about these next generations and the future of the church, as I have been amazed by the defamatory nature of some comments about the young people themselves. The assumption seems to be that any church that appeals to the interests and needs of this generation must inevitably dumb down its worship, and jettison preaching, make a commodity of itself in response to consumerism, and accommodate a self-absorption that would make Narcissus blush. The question on the minds, if not the lips, of many seems to be: "What will become of the church when we leave it to those people?"

Anxiety makes a poor counselor, and age alone makes no one wise.

I want to offer a counterplea to the assessment of many regarding the generation that is now coming of age. On the whole, this generation which has grown up high-tech is indeed much more comfortable than their elders with all things technological. My children helped me set up my iPod, and if I have a problem with a DVD player I call one of them. But the knowledge of new technologies does not mean that this generation is any less interested in deep and meaningful relationships. If they want to find the nearest coffee shop, they may turn to the Internet to get the address rather than letting their fingers do the walking through the Yellow Pages, but their love of coffee shops is less about caffeine than about community. They may be turning to "fake news" programs hosted by comedians (my children introduced me to "The Daily Show with Jon Stewart") and to online services to get their information about the world. But does anyone really think that they are missing much, if anything, by ignoring broadcast and cable news programs that are increasingly enthralled by entertainment divisions, blatantly partisan politics, and the agendas of massive global corporations that view their television newscasts primarily as venues for cross-marketing?

Some young people do enjoy contemporary worship services, and many have joined religious fellowships that are less "institutional" than the great hulking corporate systems that dominated Protestantism from 1946 to 1959. But there is also a growing interest in this generation to connect with deep, long-standing faith traditions. If anything this generation has more appreciation for participative leadership and shared governance, distrusting, as so many do, any hint of autocratic rule. There is also a remarkable resurgence among them for those forms of worship that value mystery over entrepreneurship, a fact that has left many an entrepreneurial church consultant baffled, PowerPoint pie charts not withstanding.

Among many university and college students there is also a relative lack of interest in some of the more divisive controversies that have bedeviled the church of their parents, and a correspondingly greater concern for inclusivity, openness, and transparency. As one twenty-something seminarian put it to me recently after listening to an airing of views between two church officials who differ on the ordination of practicing homosexuals: "That's your generation's issue. We're way past this."

A study reported last year by the Chronicle of Higher Education noted that the generation coming to the doors of today's colleges and universities is deeply concerned about the "big questions" of life. Far from being a generation of slackers with little thought beyond their own entertainment, I find this to be an astonishingly curious group, perhaps even more curious than their parents were. Questing for meaning, searching for answers, willing to live with a higher degree of ambiguity, sorting their way through the stunning variety of beliefs, values, cultures, faiths, and social norms that compete for their interest and allegiance, this generation deserves a church that is at least as willing to engage them and their questions as they are to engage the future. While it is unwise to be motivated by anxiety, we cannot afford to be complacent. This generation deserves a church as courageous as they long to be, a church more inspired to follow Jesus of Nazareth than to replicate the organizational chart of IBM or to define its moral superiority with the tired politics of exclusion.

For all of these reasons, I cannot think of a more valuable book for pastors, lay leaders, and anyone concerned about the future of the church than Carol Howard Merritt's *Tribal Church: Ministering to the Missing Generation*. Anyone who wants to understand better the young people who are coming to their church (or those who are not coming!) and how we can better respond to their quest for faith, meaning, life, and love should read this book, and read it with care. With profound appreciation for the ways in which God works through communities of faith, this book invites us to recover again the good news of the gospel, as George MacLeod once said, "to be to others what Christ has become for us."

Michael Jinkins
Austin Presbyterian Theological Seminary

Acknowledgments

Working on this project is a gift, especially since it allows me to contact the people who surround and embolden me with their wisdom and work. I always know that they're out there, doing great things, and usually that's enough to hearten me. But in the busyness of our lives, months and even years can slip by without contact. As I write this book, however, I have an opportunity to strengthen the bonds with many of my friends. I think of the talented and creative people whom I met in college, in seminary, and during my pastorate, and I reconnect with them through e-mails, telephone calls, and visits.

Their voices continually provoke and inspire me as I write: Beth Sentell, John Austin, Erin Echo Austin, Matthew Buell, Laura Cunningham, Liz Eide, Linda Wollschaeger Fischer, Pete Fischer, John Gage, David Gambrell, Gini Norris-Lane, Jesse Quam, Grace Davenport Quam, Scott Ramsey, Corey Sanderson, Robin Long Sanderson, Jacquline Saxon, Tara Spuhler McCabe, Erin Sharp, and Deanie Strength. For many of them, their lives and influence on me go far beyond a few quotes in a book; even with the distance between us, we've become a tribe, a sort of family.

As I began the book, John and Phyllis Wimberly motivated me to write. John, as the Head of Staff at Western Presbyterian Church, has been a perceptive mentor, giving me crucial advice and leading me to valuable resources. Our Monday morning meetings allowed me to develop the main points of the book. With John's unique balance of administrative skills and prophetic spirit, I have a working environment that many pastors would envy, and most associate pastors would be amazed to know exists: I am encouraged to name problems, communicate freely, and exercise creativity.

It's much to the credit of John's pastoral leadership that Western Presbyterian Church is such an amazing place to minister. The membership is made up of dreamers who work every day to increase peace, protect the environment, further the arts, strengthen families, heal the sick, feed the hungry, and shelter the homeless. Their concern for each other, deep love for the world, and devotion for God inspires me daily. This is my context, and I'm honored to be a part of a church where the Holy Spirit moves to make justice roll down like water, like an ever-flowing stream. I'm especially indebted to the college students and young adult class for their continual input.

A fabulous group of women are working with me on this book, the "Writing Revs," with their wondrous insight and artistry. They challenge my assumptions and give me invaluable counsel. I learn so much from them. Karen Blomberg's spiritual imagination reminds me to stay overwhelmed by God's abundance. Jan Edmiston's quick wit keeps me laughing for days, because what she says is so true. Ruth Everhart motivates me with the pace and endurance she's developed as a fine novelist. And MaryAnn McKibben's ability to compact worlds of meaning into one sentence always instructs me.

As I tied up the loose ends of the book, Linda Team and Lewis Donelson opened up their ample, warm home to me. I hope that their enlightening conversations, generous hospitality, and deep knowledge course throughout the work.

Upon completion, I have deep gratitude for the Alban Institute; for years their insightful books have nurtured me and made me a better pastor. In isolated rural settings, I could count on Alban publications to give me helpful instruction. And when I wasn't so secluded and I had a chance to speak to other church leaders, they usually referred me to Alban books as well. Alban's resourceful ministry has an astonishing impact on the church, making the body of Christ healthier and stronger. I'm grateful that they allowed me to become a part of their wonderful tradition. I thank Richard Bass and the editorial team for publishing this work. And I appreciate the keen eye and careful acumen of my editor, Ulrike Guthrie, who has the ability to make an ordinary sentence sparkle.

Of course, I want to thank my family, especially Calla and Brian, for their constant support. Calla expands my world, just with her laughter. Brian's humor and unique perspective has enriched my life for over twenty years. Brian is a tremendous husband, father, pastor, writer, and friend. That must be why we smile at each other every time Nick Lowe sings, "True love travels on a gravel road." I can't think of anyone else I'd rather be with on this bumpy, dusty, marvelous ride.

Introduction

As a child in the seventies, my family diligently attends a Southern Baptist Church on Sunday morning, Sunday night, Wednesday night, and pretty much any other time they're open. I don't mind. I love going. During the midweek program, I become intrigued by the missionary stories in my "Girls in Action" (the Baptist equivalent to Girl Scouts) handbooks. The faces of women who travel to exotic lands and help people inspire me. Even when on furlough, these missionaries tour the U.S., telling amazing stories, raising money for the next years of adventurous work. They so capture my young imagination with their tales about living in the bush, of bringing medical supplies and the good news of Jesus Christ to people around the world, that I too want to become a missionary. I imagine myself as a part of a tribe somewhere, serving as the hands and feet of Jesus.

That excitement doesn't leave me with the passing of the years, and I spend my time as a teenager going to youth group and traveling with summer mission trips. When I turn seventeen, I leave my town in Florida for the big city of Chicago, Illinois, where I enroll at the Moody Bible Institute and begin the International Ministries program.

Not long into the degree, my religious foundation crumbles. As a feminist, I believe that in Jesus Christ, "there is no Jew or Greek, slave or free, male or female." In my dorm room, I read liberation theology and am inspired by the words of Gustavo Gutiérrez who writes that people should be emancipated from those things that limit their capacity to develop themselves. Yet in my own congregation, I am not allowed to teach Sunday school to any man or boy over the age of twelve. Women

1

are considered to be equal, but they have a different role than men. It occurs to me that a "different role" would limit a woman's voice in the church, thus reducing her capability to develop herself as well as the church's potential to evolve with the essential guidance of female leadership.

As an environmentalist, I see the wonder of the world and how it reflects our beautiful Creator. I become increasingly convinced of our need to protect our water and earth from the destruction of unbridled industry and violent war. Yet in my religious life, the imminently anticipated rapture makes my conservative church unconcerned about the need for long-term stewardship.

As I work with the poor in the inner city of Chicago, providing after-school programs for children and shopping for the elderly, my economic understandings widen and my politics begin to shift. I see the importance of a society that finds ways to care for the "least of these."

As more of my friends confide to me that they are gay or lesbian, I become still more aware of my divided life. I can never reject those dearest to me, but I also can't let my closest friends step into the church where I worship, because I'm terrified of how they might hear themselves castigated by its interpretation of Scripture about sexuality.

The problem is that my viewpoints outside of my church seem much more gracious, loving, and responsible, more consistent with Christ-like behavior.

The summer before my senior year at Moody, I work in Uganda with the Anglican church and develop a voice and love for preaching. Yet, on the same trip, I become disillusioned by my intended profession when I visit a "missionary compound" in Kenya. During my brief stay, I tour a hospital and a school, and things are just as I imagined—except the complex is filled with white faces. It seems as if the missionaries have created a gated community in which they minister only to themselves. I also realize the innate racism and hypocrisy in the idea that I, as a woman, could preach and teach as much as I want to in Africa, but am not allowed to do so in the United States.

When my call into ordained ministry grows louder, I become completely torn. I know I can't live out my vocation in the conservative movement; I have to leave my evangelical roots.

Leaving the fundamentalist, evangelical church is no simple matter: it's much more than walking out one door and into another. While closing one, I am full of anxiety because the system of thought is so absolutist, so black and white, that it makes me feel like God would no longer be there at the end of it. "It's a slippery slope," my religious leaders warn me. "Once you compromise one belief, you'll lose everything."

When I enter seminary, I become the victim of some Puritan-style shunning. I have to renegotiate many friendships, as some people refuse to speak to me. The fear that my own family will reject me makes Thanksgiving gatherings almost unbearable for a while. (They never do.)

Now as I look around, I realize that I didn't make the journey alone. Many people who wept at youth Bible camps and asked Jesus into their hearts on countless occasions (we had to make sure it stuck) migrate with me: from being accepted at the altar to rejecting everything; then occasionally slipping into the back row of some church, hoping not to be noticed; and finally back into a relationship with the spiritual life, albeit an uneasy one. We who could not continue in a conservative tradition brought a great deal of pain, embarrassment, and alienation into the pews with us. We grew up while evangelicalism was at its height in the seventies and eighties, when conservatives were much better at reaching out to younger generations, when evangelicals had a passion and love for youth that I rarely found in mainline denominations.

Yet, as the seventies and eighties turned into the nineties, the conservative religious movement grew powerful in the political sphere and sexual conduct became their main focus. At the same time, many young adults grew much more progressive on social issues and sexuality, and became caught in a schism. Some conscience-driven young adults fueled the rise of "progressive evangelicalism." With a shift of emphasis to environmentalism, poverty, and hunger, activists like Jim Wallis and writers like Brian McClaren have gained an extensive audience.[1]

Others in their twenties and thirties are still searching for a space where they can nurture their connection with God and community without having to hide their progressive viewpoints. But opening a new door is not easy either. Personally, I nurtured my faith in the Presbyterian Church (USA) and for the first time, through the denomination's elders and pastors, I experienced God's grace. Of course, I didn't always feel comfortable in the mainline church, where people try to figure out where you stand on issues by gathering your resume information. I still sweat when someone asks during coffee hour where I got my undergraduate degree and I brace for their response. With my liberal stance on homosexuality (that's the dividing line in the Presbyterian Church at the moment) and my fundamentalist education, I have been viewed with suspicion by just about everyone.

Yet, I'm thankful for my path. I'm not sure how it happened, but my awkward education gave me the ability to develop congregations, even in small churches and in areas with dramatically shrinking demographics. I learned a lot from the conservative church's passion for reaching out to younger generations and from the nuts-and-bolts, practical training I received from Moody. I've heard some of the best preachers in the United States (liberals, conservatives, and everyone in between), and I've found places to minister within a mainline denominational setting with the valuable resources that I gleaned from my evangelical instruction.

Most important, by being aware of my own alienation, I have found myself much more open to God. I have learned to form some sort of community from the broken bits of younger generations. Collectively, we have found connection with God through our spiritual practices, with each other though intergenerational bonds, and with the world through social justice outreach.

I'm not alone in my final rejection of the evangelical church. I've read my own story in books like *Miss American Pie* by Margaret Sartor. I've also noticed statistics that relate a growing dissatisfaction with our country's conservative religious movement. Most people are unwilling to identify themselves as "evangelical," even when they attend evangelical churches, and conservative leaders fear that teenagers are leaving the movement in droves.[2]

I wonder where they will go. I've found great spiritual grounding and loving community in the mainline denominational church, but cracking the door has sometimes been a muscle-straining endeavor. I'm writing this book out of my own background as a twenty-year-old college student, trying to open that heavy entrance in the mainline denominational church—an experience that includes many successes and disappointments, feelings of estrangement and overwhelming mercy. I'm writing this as a pastor of growing and vibrant churches, someone who has seen great spiritual vitality in an intergenerational community. I'm writing from my experience on campuses, in working with all types of college ministries. I'm writing as a thirty-four-year-old mom, who aches with my generation over the struggles of raising children in a mire of inadequacy.

Most of all, I'm writing with enormous hope, because a generation of young, spiritual, progressive adults is wandering, looking for a home, a place where they can finally rest. Mainline denominations have tremendous resources for meeting and caring for them, and young adults have great gifts that they can offer the church. With a renewed vision and emphasis on spirituality, I pray that the mercy will continue to flow from our churches, and the Holy Spirit will give us understanding as we minister to this nomadic generation.

Generational Blockage

So, what's the problem? Every church wants those young families with two children filling their pews. They want a young man with a family as a pastor. Where's the disconnection? Why is there a shortage?

My husband, Brian Merritt, is a thirty-seven-year-old pastor who serves small churches and spent the last seven years leading congregational revitalization efforts in the Presbyterian Church (USA). At a recent seminar he taught, he referred to the Percept book, *Death of the Church*, which identified adults in their twenties and thirties as "Survivors."[3]

He introduced the term, took a deep breath, and braced himself as if he were driving into a predicted storm. Sure enough, the sky began to thunder as the familiar outrage began, "Survivors? Did you say 'Survivors?' What have they had to survive?"

"They didn't have World War II or Vietnam."

"They didn't go through the civil rights movement."

"They're recipients of unprecedented wealth!"

"I open up the real estate ads, and I can't believe how much these people will pay for a house!"

"They are so materialistic."

"You know, my nephew is still living with his parents. He's twenty-five years old."

Brian typically keeps his mouth closed during these long rants. When the storm subsides, he gently explains, "We're called Survivors because we've had to survive years of being treated like this."

He comes home after these sessions shaking his head and saying, "We are so careful in our mainline churches not to be sexist or racist, but people can be blatantly ageist, and somehow that's acceptable. I just don't understand what our generation has done that is so horrible that we have to endure so much criticism."

Maybe the ageism is acceptable in our churches because it's utterly rampant in our society. There's an idea that people under forty should never have any leadership or opinion on anything. The *Washington Post* expresses it well when it exclaims: "Ever since Clinton took the White House in '92, we've just assumed the baby boomers would hang on to power until it was pried from their cold grasp some decades hence." The article goes on to point out with great dismay a few people in their thirties who now have powerful positions. They describe their "new grown-up job" as if someone's who's 37 should not have a substantial career.[4]

Since people in their twenties and thirties hear these annoying comments so often, they often bristle under labels. There are a hundred different ways to talk about generations: The Greatest Generation, The Builders, The Boomers, The Busters, Generation X, Slackers, Adultescents, Twixters, Generation Debt, Generation Me, Generation Y, The Millenniels and Tweeners. The list goes on and on. Each tag has a great deal of research, many reports, and much sociology, marketing, and baggage attached to it. Uncomfortable with these categories, I use the general words "older" and "younger" to describe people, even though I've found many people take offense at these terms as well.

No adult likes to be called "older." In fact, last Sunday, our congregation prayed for a woman who was "ninety-two years young." Our culture has a difficult time embracing this description, at any age, but perhaps we can keep this a neutral term by thinking of it as a comparison, as in, "My seven-year-old nephew is older than my six-year-old daughter."

On the other hand, I've heard irritation and confusion over the term "younger" too. I was surprised, because I love the label and plan to hold onto it as long as I possibly can, but as I researched this book, I realized that I could be part of a small minority. One pastor complained to me, "Okay. I have kids, a mortgage, and I'm thirty-six. When will the church stop calling me young?" People get annoyed with the word's inevitable link with adolescent naivety, immaturity, and inexperience.

There is also confusion due to the marketing trend of age compression, which targets messages that were created for older children to younger ones. I recently heard a five-year-old girl protest, "I am not a child!" I was shocked. I didn't know where such an idea originated, and then I remembered the influence of our commercialized culture. Unfortunately, marketers have declared that "Kids Are Getting Older Younger" (KAGOY), so children as young as six can be considered "tweens."[5] Consequently, the "young adult" section in many large chain bookstores caters to children as young as eight years old.

With apologies, I'm going to continue the tradition of referring to adults in their twenties and thirties as "young," but I hope that I do it in a way that does not link them with other dismissive adjectives. I have banned the use of "children" and the oxymoronic term "adult children" to describe people in their twenties and thirties. Just because they are someone's offspring doesn't mean that they remain twelve for the rest of their lives.

Though no one can reflect the depth and diversity of younger generations, I offer you a snapshot from my context, from the lives of similarly aged friends, and from the situations of colleagues scattered all over the country. As we hear the voices of people in their twenties and thirties, our church can become liberated to develop our capacity and their stories can form us into vital spiritual communities.

The Tribal Church

After all these years, I do find myself ministering among tribes, although not as I had first imagined. Among a new generation, "tribe" has become a term for a subculture, a network of relationships, or a group of people who care for each other in the most basic ways. I work among urban tribes in Washington, D.C., at Western Presbyterian. Twenty years ago, 70 percent of the church membership was over seventy years old. Today the church has doubled in size and 45 percent of the adult membership is under forty-five. Our intergenerational congregation reflects years of intentional development by the pastoral staff. I describe it as a tribal church.

A tribal church has certain characteristics. It understands and reaches out to the nomadic culture of young adults. This church responds to the gifts and needs of adults under forty by taking into account their physical, social, and spiritual circumstances. The term "tribal" reflects (1) a gathering around a common cause, (2) a ministry shift to basic care, (3) the practice of spiritual traditions, and (4) a network of intergenerational encouragement.

First, tribes form around a common cause and belief. For the tribal church, we gather to connect with God. Our bonds with our Creator strengthen through worship and vital spiritual traditions, we act as the hands and feet of Jesus as we reach out to the world through social action and the care of creation, and the Holy Spirit unites us as a caring community.

Second, tribes tend to the basic needs of one another. In the same way, the tribal church realizes that young adults may require a more essential level of support. For instance, when a pastor and church leaders receive an elderly widow into the life of their congregation, they usually understand that this person will need a certain amount of care, especially if she does not have children in the area. The church members may contact her if she doesn't show up for services, invite her over for holiday meals, make sure that she has rides to her doctor's appointments, and pay attention to her general well-being.

When a young adult joins the church, we don't think of him in the same manner. We often see a healthy, strong individual who's well-off in every sense of the word. But the truth is that he might need a bit of that rudimentary care. As we'll explore in the book, adults in their twenties and thirties often do not have friends or family surrounding them in networks of support. Many of them don't have health insurance, places to spend holidays, or adequate resources. The tribal church realizes this and pays attention to the young adult's general well-being.

Third, tribes celebrate and remember traditions. Likewise, a tribal church appreciates the deep spiritual practices that form our communities. This church thrives on our best disciplines of worshiping, praying, feeding the hungry, and working for peace and justice.

Fourth, just as the bonds of a tribe depend on relationships, a tribal church is relational in nature. This church is not pastor-centered, polity-driven, or program-oriented. It is less concerned with denominational labels and hierarchy. And it doesn't follow every cultural trend that might define an edgy church. Rather, it focuses on developing an intergenerational network that allows for the viewpoints of young adults, even on controversial issues like sexuality.

Within this relational body, there's a realization that effective ministry increases with the intention to share power with a new generation. So the members of a tribal church work to counsel, guide, train, and enable young leaders.

Many growth movements geared toward young adults seem unattainable for church leaders, unless they're planting a new congregation. In the midst of this exciting conversation, I hope to give voice to those who don't want to worship in a coffeehouse, and don't want their sanctuary to turn into one. There are young adults who enjoy worshiping in an intergenerational setting, who can't imagine giving up the beauty of having children and elders look for Easter eggs together. I speak for those who cherish the rich art, liturgy, and music that have expressed our soaring praise and our deepest lamentations for centuries. For those who love to sneak into an empty church sanctuary just to hear their footsteps echo, feel the cold ancient walls, and listen for those saints who somehow remain present. There are those who are still inspired by the beauty and poetry of sermons from ages past; they don't find them inauthentic or irrelevant.

There is a new generation looking for spiritual community, and many of them are looking for small to medium, traditional churches. May we have the understanding to reach out to them, and may they be able to open our church doors with ease.

CHAPTER I

Tribal
Church

In my bedroom, I have a Gabbeh rug, woven in deep browns and greens. Not the typical elegant Persian rug, this one has thick choppy wool, rough edges, and crooked lines. Made with vegetable dyes, each row changes colors, leaving a wonderful earthy richness. In a region known for its fine and intricate carpets, these rugs are bottom of the line because they are constructed and carried by nomadic tribes who pack them on animals until they set down a temporary home, then unfold them onto the ground, where their family can gather on that four by six-foot area.

I imagined it would be comforting to have a bit of familiar space to unpack upon reaching a strange land. That's why I bought the carpet. I entered the store, Peaceable Kingdom, in Providence, Rhode Island, just after accepting a call to be a pastor in Washington, D.C. Thrilled about my new position, I had no doubt that God had called me there, but at the same time, I loved my church in Rhode Island and did not want to move from the beautiful New England town where we lived.

To work through my confusing grief, I sought the kind company of Joan and Phil Ritchie, a couple of Episcopalian anthropologists who owned a shop crammed full of precious artistic pieces from all over the globe. Entering the store was like entering another world. The items inside held the faint smell of dust and roaming animals and they created the sense that resourceful people could fashion art from anything.

The eclectic assortment of artifacts reflected the Ritchie's full lives, crowded with interesting and unique stories. Feeling like a treasure hunter, each time I surveyed the store's stock I found some eccentric piece tucked in a corner. "Is this new?" I would ask, holding up a two-foot mask, lightly caked in dust.

"Oh no. We've had that for years. I'm not sure why it hasn't sold." Then Joan would spend the next few minutes telling a fascinating story about a festival in Mexico that they had attended and the missionary influence in that region. As she spoke, my eyes gravitated to the rugs. While preparing to put our house on the market in preparation for our move to D.C., I realized I needed a carpet to cover the shiny wood flooring my husband and I had recently installed.

As if I had just entered a bazaar in Turkey, the owners saw my attention shifting and sprung into action, unrolling rugs that were leaning against the side wall and pulling out interesting weavings from the piles in the center of the room. Since half of my household furnishings had come from that store, they knew my taste well and introduced me to that beautiful Gabbeh carpet.

The owner hesitated a bit when she saw my excitement, and I could tell that she was not quite ready to let the rug go, but she continued to explain its rich history with the nomadic tribes, pointing out that the weavers kept with their Islamic tradition and left out the images of flowers and animals more popular with Western buyers. So as I got ready to move for the seventh time in sixteen years, I bought the carpet and packed it into the trunk of my car. I needed a familiar space that I could take with me, something that was sturdy, warm, and not likely to wear out anytime soon.

I don't travel with a caravan of extended family and friends, but like many in my generation of thirty-somethings, I move often with my spouse and daughter, increasingly away from my family of origin.[1] When I unpacked my boxes in Arlington, Virginia, I rolled out the rug in my bedroom. My daughter and I sat down on the thick pile as we listened to books on tape and admired the brown and green diamond shapes. The soft itchiness tickled my hands, connecting me to my history in Rhode Island, as well as its own years of tradition tightly wound up into its threads.

Urban Tribes

The carpet reminds me that each place I find myself, I try to quickly set up a little area where I can meet friends and gather a makeshift family. Sometimes it is an actual space in a coffeehouse or church, other times I gather with people around community arts or a political movement. After roaming across the country for education and jobs in my own nomadic pattern, I have learned to do this as a survival technique.

Evidently, even though I feel dreadfully alone sometimes, I'm not alone. Ethan Watters wrote an article about meeting his young unmarried friends every Tuesday night at a particular restaurant and labeled them an "urban tribe." From the outpouring of mail the little piece received, he realized that the sociological trend was widespread, so he wrote a book on this development.[2]

The term "urban tribe" strikes a chord with me too, although I'm married and have a child. Away from my family of origin, I long for community. As a pastor, I see that the best work of our church springs up when these groups begin to form: small, cohesive parties who can depend on each other for interesting friendships, pet sitting, and meaningful holidays. When someone plans to heat up some leftovers from the freezer for Thanksgiving dinner, a few members of the group call and suddenly it seems worthwhile to invest in the entire turkey. When a person is about to spend Christmas Eve with a bottle of red wine and an extended visit to her Facebook site, she abruptly realizes that she can meet some flesh and blood friends at a candlelight service. When a young adult feels like Easter is less of a celebration of resurrection and more of a fertility ritual pointing out that he has no children for whom to hide eggs, he figures out that he can get together for brunch with other single thirty-year-olds after the sunrise service.

Forming Tribal Churches

When I began as a twenty-seven-year-old pastor of a small rural church, ministering to young adults seemed like an impossible task, especially when I looked at newspapers, philosophy, and church growth trends. Newspapers and magazines often dressed young adults up as greedy slackers, ever-sponging off our parents and never assuming responsible roles in society.[3] They looked down that deep hole of debt and wondered how students could ever justify their computers, iPods, and expensive coffees.

I often did not recognize the people our popular culture described. Even in their most noble struggles, younger generations were portrayed as a bunch of naïve youth who did not really know what they were protesting against. No matter what cause united moms, how much volunteering dads engaged in, or what trends twenty-year-olds began, they were inevitably compared disparagingly to Baby Boomers, the civil rights movements of the sixties, and were eternally dwarfed in that Boomer-looming shadow. How could the church understand young adults if it continually looked at them through the tinted spectacles of older adults?

As I encountered postmodern philosophy and studied Michel Foucault and Luce Irigaray, Jacques Derrida and Julia Kristeva, I began to comprehend the inadequacy of language, the fallibility of institutions, the distinction of the self, and the relativity of truth, but it rarely helped me move the church forward in concrete ways in ministry with young adults. In fact, in the midst of postmodernism, I was often left with the doomed feeling that I would never understand anything, *especially* the current intellectual movements.

Then I read church growth material, which thoughtfully categorized younger generations. I loved studying books like *Soul Tsunami*, but when I tried to put some ideas into practice in my elderly congregation (like the instructions to "get glocal"), I realized the great gulf between where we were as a church and where we needed to be to implement the suggested ideas. I began swimming and swirling, feeling hopeless, like I had to reinvent two thousand years of solid traditions and practice to reach out to my generation.[4]

Plus, the more I read about younger generations in the mainline church and looked through conference materials, the more I noticed that my viewpoints were being described by people who looked suspiciously like they came from the same vintage as my mom and dad.

Visiting contemporary worship services particularly designed for young adults made me feel irritated and empty. I was a part of a large, growing segment of spiritual young adults who wanted nothing to do with contemporary worship. I grew up attending conservative megachurches and had friends who left the Christian music scene. They told me so many stories about the industry and the people who wrote those catchy verses that the songs went down like bad sausage. As soon as I saw that white screen slither down from the ceiling, I knew that I was going to have a difficult time stomaching the next twenty-five minutes. Someone was trying too hard to be hip. Like my high school English teacher's attempts to be fashionable and cool, it just seemed *wrong*.

I was being unfair. Actually I think that I was just jealous. Obviously, there was a place in our society for slick worship, but I was like most pastors. I could never be hip, even when I tried really, really hard. I could buy a pair of designer jeans to wear on a Sunday morning and use the word "awesome" a lot, but I was still perfectly square (and yes, I knew that use of the terms "hip" and "square" illustrated my point).

My rural church was far from cool too. It was small, ancient, and full of people over sixty—and the perfect place to effectively care for young adults. Like those nomadic tribes, our church needed a rug—a comforting space for young adults, a place where years of tradition formed something beautiful. And they came, and they began to join. Over time, we began to weave a rich tapestry of diverse, intergenerational people. We did not discover the formula for a booming Gen X megachurch in just three years; instead, we reversed the trend of lost membership, kept the original members, and had a consistent ten percent growth made up of individuals of various ages. Our congregation became an intergenerational meeting ground, a place for supportive tribes to form, and I began to realize that our mainline denominational church has great assets for reaching out to young adults. When I moved to Rhode Island, I noticed the same thing happened in that bayside New England town of Barrington. Then I joined the staff of Western Presbyterian Church, an urban church in Washington, D.C., where the flow of young members seemed to rise every week.

Weaving Connections

Though young adults came, we realized how easy it was for them not to. It's no longer important for someone in their twenties or thirties to go to church. With a subscription to the Sunday *New York Times* and plenty of morning news programs, a person has stacks of weekend entertainment right in her own home. "Meeting a nice young man" is no incentive, since many contacts are now made in bars or over the Internet. Denominational affiliation has very little power in our politics or workplaces. The societal expectation to attend worship is gone, the blue laws faded a long time ago, and now children have plenty of sporting and scouting opportunities during those once-sacred hours.

When a young person walks into a church, it's a significant moment, because no one expects her to go and nothing pressures her to attend; instead, she enters the church looking for something. She searches for connection in her displacement: connection with God through spiritual practices, connection with her neighbors through an intergenerational community, and connection with the world through social justice outreach.

The church has been making these vital connections for thousands of years, and we can easily respond to the young, weary travelers in our midst, letting them know that they can find a spiritual home within our worshiping communities and that we will provide a supportive space for them so that they can form their tribe.

Our churches can weave a source of connection. I have seen tribes gather in a variety of settings: in a college town, the rural countryside, a New England community, and an urban setting. Watching relations and groups develop in a church, creating and maintaining space for them, is a vital part of what I do as a pastor.

Envisioning what the church will look like in the next twenty years, I imagine a body that gathers together to worship God, strives for social justice, and cultivates tribes. In the following chapters, I look at how we can develop:

1. Intergenerational relationships
2. Economic understanding

3. Unambiguous inclusion
4. Affirming traditions
5. Shared leadership
6. Spiritual guidance

In the chapters two and three, I explore the general milieu in which young adults live, especially the sense of isolation that results from generational divisions and economic instability. In chapters four, five, and six, I look at the specific ways in which people in their twenties and thirties can feel estranged from our congregations, especially focusing on the unfortunate consequences of the church's exclusive beliefs, customs that cut off a new generation, and hesitance to share power. Throughout the book, I offer solutions to many of the problems. In chapter seven, I draw attention to the place where the longing of young adults and the gifts of the church converge: the cultivation of spiritual guidance and development of caring communities.

Even the smallest churches—*especially* the smallest churches— have the resources to respond to young adults in meaningful ways when they understand their contexts and make a place for them. These relationships take shape when our intergenerational groups of displaced families and single people begin to weave a rich tapestry of familiar space.

Reflection Questions

1. With a map of the world and colored pencils, have each person in your group draw a line for each place he or she has lived. Be sure to include when you have lived in a place for a month or more, working with the church, serving in the military, studying abroad, etc. If it's a small group, each person can explain why he or she moved in each instance. If it's a large group, you can divide up and this exercise can be done with two to four people.
2. How many people moved in their lifetime? Who moved the most? What did it feel like when you unpacked your boxes? What was your first holiday away from your family like? How did you find friends? Relate a story about moving into a new area.

3. When moving to a new place, how did you find a church? What did the church do to make you feel welcome there? Do you remember what happened that made you decide to worship there?

4. What about the church you're currently worshiping in? What attracted you to the congregation? What does your church do well when welcoming new people?

CHAPTER 2

Fostering Intergenerational Relationships

Marsha earned a PhD in engineering. Some years later, she left her teaching job, moved to another state, and became a stay-at-home mom. In her new surroundings, she missed the intellectual stimulus of her academic setting and found that she did not have many friends. It didn't take Marsha long to get connected with playgroups and library programs in her town where she met other moms, but finding a church proved to be more difficult. As her family visited different worshiping communities, Marsha was on the lookout for a large, program-oriented church, with a lot of parents her age and plenty of activities for her child. But much to her own surprise, she settled on a small denominational church.

Why?

Although dissatisfied that there were not more programs for her child, and although she had set out to find a congregation with people her age, Marsha found herself needing the support that she was getting from the older women. "You just can't imagine how it feels for me to be at home all week with my child. I don't think I'm doing anything right, and then I come to church, and one of the grandmothers tells me how good Rachel is. They always let me know that I'm a good mom, that I'm doing a good job. I don't get that anywhere else."

When Marsha had her second child, the women in her church made up a detailed schedule for themselves so that someone was always on call and prepared to support Marsha in the early days and weeks. They surrounded her with care, making sure that her oldest daughter had someone to stay with from the time Marsha went into labor until the child's grandmother could make it into town. Even as a new resident in a strange town, an intergenerational tribe grew up around her. Marsha knew that no matter what time of the day or night it was, she could call on this faithful group of women to assist her.

Although these caring women were particularly helpful, this story is not unusual. The fabric of our churches is so strong and durable that when one thread grows thin, we can rely on the many others surrounding it to keep things together. Many times, we find that assistance from generations other than our own.

A House Divided Against Itself

We need and yearn for intergenerational connection. Yet in our culture, our lives are more and more divided based on age. Singer and songwriter John Austin says, "We get entertainment and noise everywhere. We're always around our own kind." While older people may watch the nightly news, younger generations get their information from the Internet. Television producers gear programs toward target audiences, so much that we not only find a simple distinction between adult and children's programming while navigating through the channels, we find discrete shows for infants, toddlers, children, tweens, and teenagers. My sixty-year-old friends can't comprehend that my favorite shows are usually adult cartoons and fake documentaries, but I can't understand how a person comes home after a hard day's work and watches an exhausting hour-long drama.

We not only have a variety of music, but we collect it in a different ways: buying a CD has become a nostalgic act now that most twenty-year-olds download their music. I read the sad news that the Tower Records store near the George Washington University campus closed. That would have been unimaginable when I was in college. While I shop for a stereo and plenty of CD storage, the college students I work with buy MP3 players and carry virtually thousands of tunes in the palms of their hands.

Even the way in which our phones ring is distinctive, packaged and marketed to us based on our age. Teenagers figured out that older ears have more difficulty hearing higher frequencies, so companies developed a ring tone that typically only people under thirty can hear. Now students can text each other during class without the teacher ever noticing.[1]

Although grateful for such a variety of music and entertainment, I'm concerned that broader generational divides will tear into the fabric of our society just as intergenerational care becomes more and more crucial. I'm worried that we will keep buying products which make it harder for us to hear each other.

Church growth trends that market specifically to younger generations while ignoring the elderly, and congregations who care for older members while neglecting young adults, exacerbate the schisms in our society. The church is one place where we can still have multi-generational interaction, and it is crucial for the fabric of our society to preserve, maintain, and enhance this connection. Indeed, as John Austin says, "The healthiest islands are biodiverse."

In our increasingly segregated culture, older generations, young families, and single people can learn to listen and care for each other. Mainline denominational congregations can increase intergenerational hospitality through visible signs so growth can flourish and we can expand our biodiversity.

OLDER GENERATIONS

The segregation of our society spills over from our entertainment into most aspects of our everyday lives. Older people tend to be isolated in child-free condos, retirement communities, and nursing facilities, so we have less interaction with each other. Understandably, living independently and not being a burden on one's children is a goal for many elderly people, and our culture is in the midst of negotiating what this will look like as people live longer. At this time, grandmothers and grandfathers rarely move to live in the same home with their sons, daughters, and grandchildren; instead, we see an increase in long-term care facilities. Even when they enter residential care, people don't always move into the same town with their sons or daughters. It often doesn't make sense to them to follow their mobile offspring from place to place; they would rather find ways to remain in their hometown, where their friends and support reside. In many ways these are wonderful trends, giving people more independence and freedom to choose their living environments and the extent of long-term care.

Yet, this separation in our culture causes us to miss the insight, history, and perspective of older generations. When contact with the elderly decreases, we become less in touch with their physical, emotional, and social needs, and in turn our own views of life, sickness, and death become gravely distorted. Our own ideas about living and growing old become unclear. The cartoon caricatures of older adults that our children see on television are blue-haired and muumuu-clad. They speak with grating, gravelly voices, and are typically found hunched over a walker. Worst of all, they are usually insufferably dim-witted. These popular personalities are a far cry from the realities of the vital, wise elderly people who inhabit our churches.

Conversely, older people miss the vital company and hope that young adults and children can provide. Our empathy dulls when we do not communicate with other generations: resentment festers, stereotypes grow, and our society suffers from the misunderstandings of an ageist culture.

Grace Slick, the singer and songwriter who started her career in the psychedelic rock of the sixties, deftly sums up an ageist sentiment when she says, "Old people should be heard and not seen. Young people should be seen and not heard."[2]

In contrast, in the church, we want the old, the young, and everyone in between to be seen and heard. Communication between generations will become even more vital as more people retire in the coming decade. For increasingly retirement does not equal ease of living. Currently, close to one-third of retirement-aged people have no assets saved and more than two-thirds of retirees rely on Social Security for half or more of their living expenses. Fifty-three percent of workers aged fifty-five to sixty-four have no retirement savings account at all and the ones who do have a median balance of $25,000. An unfortunate result of the high divorce rate in the 1970s is that single parents are even less likely to be ready for retirement.[3] As health care, prescriptions, and long-term care costs increase, millions of people will be living beyond their assets, and younger generations will need to assume more responsibility for their parents.

Our days of single-family living may soon come to an end, as adult sons and daughters will need to convert their extra bedrooms into apartments for their parents. These large-scale adjustments will not occur without a great deal of communication, and since the church is one of the last places where the young and old still gather together it is a community we do well to nurture and celebrate. Because the fabric of our society depends on intergenerational tribes, it is in everyone's interests to guard, maintain, and nourish those connections between older adults, young families, and single people.

We give each other an invaluable gift of perspective when we talk to each other. At one time, I was incessantly badgering my parents about their health, caught in an irritating cycle, wondering why they never listened to me. Then, I discussed the matter with Joan, a retiree with a grown son and daughter. When I stopped to take a breath, she asked me, "Carol, do you like it when your parents instruct you about how to raise your child?" My mom has never done anything like that, but I could imagine how it would feel if she did.

"Well, it feels the same way when you nag them about their health."

Suddenly, the family dynamics made sense to me. I finally understood my parents' perspective and I remembered, once again, the importance of the intergenerational connection in my church. Presumably many conversations like that one will occur in the years to come, as our nation begins caring for an aging population.

YOUNG FAMILIES

It can be a scary thing to be a parent, to raise children. A parent finds a strange rash and wants to rush straight to the emergency room. It's unnerving when it takes more than twenty minutes to potty train a two year old. And with all of the educational tools available for infants, it seems like children should be prepared to take the SAT by the time they're five.

Unfortunately, the culture of young parents can be difficult. When moms and dads gather together, they have expectations for themselves and for each other to have incredible birthday parties, the finest educational opportunities, and extensive extracurricular involvement for their children. Their schedules have to fit around nap times and sports, so it can be months before they can schedule a play date into their palm pilots. For some reason, it's easy to get lost in perfectionism even when knee deep in diapers. Judith Warner, the author of *Perfect Madness: Motherhood in the Age of Anxiety,* writes about "the mess" in which middle-class mothers find themselves. She explains that this generation is caught up in a society where many of them do not live at the economic level of their parents, yet it's a "hypercompetitive and excruciatingly expensive age," where they put everything into their children, hoping to make them winners, knowing that "unless they succeed, they might not have a foothold on the Good Life." [4]

The stress doesn't end with children; we put pressure on ourselves to have it all together: our homes, the sports, the vacations, and the parent-teacher involvement. There is not a single aspect of our lives that we can let go.

I know I get caught up in all of it, trying to be the perfect mom and homemaker on top of balancing the perfect career. A friend recently asked for a tour of "my garden." I led her through the row of hostas which stood in front of the row of azaleas, and I could tell she expected more. So I took her into the back yard where the ivy, wildflowers, and three more azalea bushes grew. My neighbor had morning glories that climbed over our chain link fence and ate one of our bicycles, entangling the spokes in their glorious vinery. I loved the flowers so I just couldn't bear to cut them back until they stop blooming.

Stepping by the hopeless, hidden weed patch on the side yard, I noticed that it'd been recently decorated with a languishing kiddie pool and I flushed with embarrassment. Pages from *Southern Living* magazine haunted me with their perfect peonies and lovely lilacs. I remembered that I had never gotten around to mulching or fertilizing this year and suddenly everything looked overgrown or wilted. I began apologizing, making excuses, and mumbling something about hiring a landscaper.

Until I finally stopped and made a mental note to myself, "Wait a second. You have a full-time job and you're a mom. You don't have to have a perfect garden. Overgrown azaleas residing in last year's mulch are just fine." In my anxiety, I realized the dewy manna on my bedraggled lawn. At those hungry times when we feel like we can never be enough, we are reminded that God gives us what we need, and those small mercies are new every morning.

As moms and dads, we can get caught up in perfectionism. With the endless self-help and parenting books available at our bookstores, we have learned well that what we do matters in the development of our children. And somehow that knowledge can develop from healthy attachment into an unhealthy narcissism in which our children become an extension of who we are. Their behavior becomes our shame or our reward. Too much fear and guilt can turn nurturing, responsible parents into hovering, stressed-out control freaks.

Since our own moms and dads may live thousands of miles away, we often do not have the perspective that older parents have, and when we spread ourselves too thin with our worry and obsession, it's amazing to sense that interweaving connection with older generations. They often give us the manna that we need.

I've experienced this on many occasions. One time, I was making a pastoral visit with Parker, a father and grandfather, and I had something gnawing in the back of my mind. I was worried about my three-year-old daughter's active imagination: she didn't seem to be able to distinguish fact from fiction. It was a typical stage that children go through, one that my little girl quickly outgrew, but I didn't know it at the time.

Parker could sense my distraction, so he asked me about it. I settled down for a couple hours of psychological analysis and soul-searching, getting ready to dive into the depths of my past so that we could illuminate my character defects and come up with a long list of things that I should be doing as a parent to keep this from happening.

Parker's reply was a little different from the ones that I normally got from my thirty-year-old friends, though. He responded, "Well, there's an easy solution to that one. You need to have another baby, and then you'll quit obsessing over this one so much." Having another baby didn't sound like an easy solution to me, but it did help me to laugh, have some perspective in my situation, and be grateful for the wisdom of the older people in our church.

At Western Presbyterian Church in Washington, D.C., we met in a women's spirituality group where the rich intergenerational nature of the class was its most precious asset. When Lisa, a woman in the group, became pregnant, we gathered quotes together, sentences that were important to us, funny sayings, bits of good sense and prayers that we relied on as mothers and grandmothers. One night Lisa missed a meeting, so we raided the Sunday school supply closet for paper, glitter, and glue sticks, and decorated the wisdom into a stack of lovely cards to give to the new mom.

While we assembled the notes, the grandmothers laughed at all the things they thought were so important when their children were growing up. "Now, as a grandparent, all of that stuff just seems so trivial," one woman thoughtfully told us as she shared her perspective of time. We discussed the significance and beauty of the relationship between grandparents and grandchildren, and I became more aware of this unique bond. Through this simple exercise, we created a connection with and a rite of passage for this new mom, so she knew that she had support from a wide range of women from their twenties to their sixties that she could rely upon as her son grew.

YOUNG SINGLES

Yet, when we minister to younger generations, we must go beyond caring for the needs of young families. Someone in his twenties or thirties is probably not married with children, nor living with a partner, but most likely single. However, we often don't acknowledge single people in our congregations. "Church is like Noah's ark," a young widow explained to me. "People expect you to enter two-by-two."

This notion changes as we spend more energy with adults in their twenties and thirties. When we reach out to younger generations, we become aware that people marry later now; in fact, the median age for a person's first marriage is at a historic highpoint and the marriage rate is decreasing. [5]

A clearer understanding of this reality will take more time than many pastors are now investing. When solo and senior pastors were asked, "In your ministry in the congregation, with which age groups do you spend most of your time working?" even when they were allowed to select two age categories, a meager 4 percent of mainline Protestants pastors reported that they spend their time working with single young adults; in comparison, 69 percent spend their time with older adults.[6]

Growth in a particular age group takes attention, and our mainline denominational churches spend fewer hours on young single people than any other group. When a young man slips into the pew alone, he is also slipping through the cracks in our supposedly caring congregations. Robert Putnam, the author of *Bowling Alone*, notices this trend of absent single people in our congregations when he points out the "life-cycle" pattern in our churches, "Generally speaking, marriage and children encourage greater involvement in church activities. In addition, middle aged and older people . . . seem more drawn to religion than are younger people." [7]

We often think of singleness as something temporary, a stage that a person goes through before she "settles down." We think of her not so much as being single as simply not yet married, and we ignore the particular situations of gays and lesbians. With these fuzzy delineations, single people hardly exist in the consciousness of our congregations. As a result, congregations overlook the needs and gifts of this important group and give them about 4 percent of our attention at a time when they just might require the connection with a congregation the most.

Single people often have a flood of relationship, career, and financial decisions to make. Since jobs are more abundant in urban areas, single people often move there, but rents are substantially higher. So, young single professionals are in a precarious position, trying to pay off their student loans and credit cards at the same time as paying high rents. Young couples want to become financially stable before they get married, but often financial stability demands two incomes. It's a pernicious cycle.

More and more, people are choosing to be single, without children. And young singles have learned to build tribes, relying on friends and forming long-lasting relationships. They have a great deal to show the church about community and caring for one another, if only we will stop ignoring them and begin building intergenerational connections in our congregations.

YOUNG COUPLES

Couples without children are another group that's underrepresented. Although churches often design their programs to attract married couples with children, only 10 percent of American households actually have that arrangement.[8] In our society, not everyone wants to have children; yet, childfree couples often endure small slights in their families of origin, like holidays that revolve around their fertile siblings. In a church service, for a couple who wishes they can have children, every Sunday can feel like Mother's Day as well-meaning people probe, "So, when are you going to start a family?" It's an innocent question, but for a husband and wife who've been trying for years to have kids, the question stings.

For Jim, who lives with his wife, Ann, in a small town in Ohio, it's been a particularly painful experience: "Couples without children—and I know many—are underrated in the church," Jim writes. In their struggle with infertility, they went to clinics and underwent all sorts of test, but they were not been able to get pregnant.

During that difficult time, their sorrow became more profound as they attended church. Their spiritual community was a harmful environment for them. "We've found the church almost totally un-equipped to deal with the issue of a couple who wants to have children but hasn't been able. We started young. We fashioned our lives around the hope of having children." Yet, within the church, they were con-sidered "selfish" because they enjoyed their lives as a couple. No one seemed to understand it was out of their control; they just couldn't have children. Finally, they learned to quit hoping, stop expecting, and not think about it.

Many people in their twenties and thirties (married and single) live with the grief and pain of infertility. Their arms ache for the warmth of a sleeping child, and they feel a profound emptiness at not being able to have children. With our church's care of and emphasis on kids and families, we cannot forget those who cannot have children, and we must be mindful of their difficulties. These are the things that never make it to the prayer list in our congregations, but the burden and loss of it all still sits in the pews.

Furthermore, same-sex couples make up one in nine unmarried couples in our country.[9] While our nation grapples with the idea of same-sex marriage, this can become a fruitful time to begin understand-ing the difficulties that many lesbian and gay couples face when they try to adopt a child, secure health insurance, or visit a partner in intensive care. As the debate unfolds on the national stage, we can tune our ears to the particular necessities of same-sex couples and understand that their relationships require particular encouragement and nurture in a society that is often hostile to them.

The hardships that same-sex couples face can even exist if a relationship ends. In the case that a long-term relationship dissolves, the heart-breaking difficulties of dividing an estate and determining custody can heighten without legal advice. If a relationship ends with a death, the grieving spouse or partner can be completely ignored by the pastor, by the blood relatives, in an obituary, or during a funeral service. Then, the surviving spouse or partner often has an extremely difficult time inheriting property, and the grief can intensify.

Visible Signs of Hospitality

When intergenerational bonds flourish, they can be invaluable. Each time we take the children Christmas caroling at the nursing home, we bring joy to the residents and we instruct children about how our elderly neighbors live, thus increasing empathy and contact between generations. Each time a retired person explains the particular challenges of their financial situation to a career starter, it reminds him to plan for the future. This understanding will be vitally important if current trends continue in the years to come.

Intergenerational communication works against the movements in our popular culture. When I was growing up in the 1970s, a subtle shift occurred in advertising and marketing, and that simple five-degree turn set our culture on a path that is miles away from its original course. Television commercials began addressing children, rather than their parents, about buying toys. Corporations realized that they could begin "branding" children at a young age.[10] Since then, younger generations have been directly and boldly marketed to, and they have become highly aware of when a package is for them and when it is for their parents.

Even though we congregations may not like to think of ourselves as marketing packages, we are stuck in this distorted system, and it is clear for anyone in their twenties or thirties that most of our denominational churches are packaged toward older generations. Worshiping bodies may not have a conscious promotional agenda, but as a part of a highly consumeristic society, we portray ourselves as a place for old people. So as younger people "shop around" for a church, they might see that we have a Sunday school program and a smattering of things for children, but too often church leadership, social events, and fundraisers are geared toward people who are over sixty.[11] In our highly segregated and ageist culture, younger generations get the message that since the church is for another generation, then it's not for their children, and it's definitely not for them.

In implicit and explicit ways, we communicate to children, youth, young adults, and families that the church isn't for them. For instance, if we look at the church parlor, we may find a beautiful array of furniture: comfortable couches, shiny cherry wood end tables, and lovely curtains. It is an inviting place for grown ups to relax, sip some coffee, and discuss important matters.

Then, if we wander into the nursery, we might find something completely different. There's a crib in the corner, and the bars are so far apart that you can fit a pumpkin through them. The curtains are faded and the pulls on the blinds are dangling dangerously. The toys are a collection of attic rejects, bits and pieces of nostalgic antiquities. Parents may walk in and begin calculating how much money the church could make selling those weeble wobbles on eBay, but they hardly want their children playing with them. The Sunday school rooms have cabinets filled with faded construction paper, broken crayons, and dried up markers.

We communicate implicit messages when the sanctuary and other grown-up spaces are well kept and pleasant yet we send our children off to stale dungeons to learn about Jesus. Unfortunately, these are lessons that people keep with them throughout their lives. Ana June, a contributor to *Breeder: Real-Life Stories from the New Generation of Mothers*, writes her "Confessions of a Heathen":

> When I was still young enough to attend Sunday school, I once went to a church with my grandparents. I remember little from the experience, except this: The Sunday-school room smelled like barf. Strongly, deeply like barf. And everyone, kids included, tried to pretend that all was normal. There we were, singing and playing churchy games in a barfy room, and there was absolutely no missing that odor. No mistaking it.[12]

Many churches recognize the message that they send to their community, so they begin a radical shift to incorporate contemporary music, reaching out to young adults with expensive and slick advertising campaigns. This often works, and many congregations have taken huge risks by incorporating younger generations into their worshiping communities, but they often alienate older members while they attract young members.

The other problem with this solution is that Barbie has been wooing younger generations for decades. Adults in their twenties and thirties have been marketed to all of their lives and they are weary of it. Feeling manipulated and used, they long for authentic signs of hospitality. When a Starbucks opens up in the fellowship hall, a dad might enjoy a four dollar latte, but he knows that he has been the target of marketing and the double skim will quickly sour in his stomach. Young adults don't want to be a target audience and don't want to be labeled as "Generation X," especially in their spiritual communities.

Ironically, many adults in their thirties reject products that are marketed to older generations and products that are marketed toward them. They don't want to belong to a focus group; they want spiritual depth, affirming traditions, and welcoming spaces. So they look for thoughtful signs of caring and visible bridges of hospitality that grow up when a worshiping community becomes intentional about ministering to younger generations.

When congregations want to gather an intergenerational tribe, they do well to review their space with an eye to deliberately incorporating what young adults will find welcoming. A church communicates hospitality beyond the nametag, handshake, and smile at coffee hour; many small things signal to a young person whether she belongs there. We can provide caring environments for all people from the cradle to the grave, without neglecting what's in between. We can look through the eyes of families and singles to build demonstrations of warm reception.

FAMILIES

A young mother, Lisa, held her two-year-old daughter's hand as she told me about her search for a church in her new home in Maine. She came from a conservative Baptist congregation, and her family chose to join a liberal Episcopal church.

"Why'd you pick that church?" I asked, perplexed by her theological turnabout.

"Because they had Purell dispensers on the wall of the nursery," was her matter-of-fact answer. I was startled by the seeming shallowness of this intelligent woman's answer; but as I thought about it more, I realized that the Purell dispenser said something important about how her child would be cared for and treated in that place. It was a small implicit sign of welcome. We can be intentional about those symbols as we carefully look for ways to broaden our hospitality, letting every generation know that they are welcome.

Congregations have a variety of ways to communicate hospitality to people of all generations. To begin, it will be important to make the buildings accessible, so that physical limitations will not keep a person from attending. When the Americans with Disabilities Act passed requiring wheelchair access, many congregations put off the additional structural changes because of the tremendous cost. Now, years later, the expense has only increased and our buildings lag far behind acceptable standards; yet our worshiping communities need the ramps and widened doorways more than ever. As people live longer, they are more likely to remain active even when they lose their mobility. Anyone who is disabled or has a disabled loved one knows just how difficult it is to maneuver in a building with narrow stairs, small entrances, and inadequate restrooms. Instead, we can be on the forefront of society, as a welcoming, fully inclusive, and fully accessible church.

As a congregation begins to create an intergenerational space, they might imagine their congregation as newly pregnant. Even if you have no children in your church, even if you do not have anyone of childbearing age gathering for worship, you can create a hopeful space. Faithful communities are really good at this: we have an entire season for this purpose. So we can establish Advent in the church, making sure that the space has been prepared for the children who are to come. Just as a young couple begins a nesting period, a church can begin making sure that the facilities are safe and welcoming for children.

Walk through your church with a safety-conscious mom or dad and ask them to point out the issues that your building might have.

Make a checklist of all of the cabinets that need latches, outlets that need covers, and cords that need to be bundled. Become aware of how the church stores cleaning supplies and where they keep the kitchen knives. See if there's a clean, safe space for a parent to change an infant's diapers or for a mom to nurse her baby. Imagine how a dad would take his two-year-old daughter to the restroom in the church's facilities.

Go through the toy boxes in the nursery and sort through the dolls and trains. Most parents will point out unacceptable or worrisome toys. The parents in our church nursery sorted out all of the tiny parts ("choking hazards"), all of the old painted blocks ("lead poisoning"), and all of the plush stuffed animals ("germ factories"). The Barbies ("too sexual") and the weaponry ("too violent") were also tossed. In their place, the parents supplied the nursery with new things that could easily be thrown into a dishwasher. They bought modern books that presented a multi-cultural world, replacing the strangely Swedish-looking Jesus found in the older Bible stories.

As we begin to look at our worship and educational spaces with the eyes of people with particular requirements, we can envision what else a small child would need: stepstools in the restrooms or drawing pads in the pews. A tiny rural congregation in Dixie Belcher, Louisiana, recognized that just as families are more likely to eat at restaurants that provide a kids' menu and something to color, so they could make church more appealing by providing worship bags for the children, filling them with children's bulletins and crayons. They began with two or three simple totes, now they have dozens.

By extension, each time the doors of the church open, we can imagine what would make church more inviting or even simply what would make it possible for various people with different needs to attend. That means, for example, planning for the possibility of children participating in every event. How might we enable that to happen? Instead of shying away from offering childcare because of the expense, why not offer it precisely so that those with children would not be hindered from attending church? If we want younger generations involved in our churches, we can make it a goal that every time the church doors are open, we will provide care for people of every age or ability. That does not mean that childcare will always be needed, but the bulletin announcement and the nominating committee's invitation can at least communicate that childcare can be arranged.

I have spoken to parents who told me privately that the reason they turned down the nomination to become an elder or a deacon was simply that they could not afford a babysitter. If we want younger people on our governing bodies, then we have to be one step ahead of their calculations. We can begin thinking about their needs, and the interconnected requirements of an entire family: for young children, elderly parents, mentally ill loved ones, or mentally challenged siblings.

Singles

But inclusion is not just about children and parents. Fostering tribal community means we cannot neglect single people but should intentionally nurture community for those who are students, career starters, widowed, gay, lesbian, or bisexual. We can become mindful of single people of all ages.

When Western Presbyterian Church wanted to focus on young single adults, they recognized that a person likes to walk into a sanctuary and see other people like herself in the church. So, to increase the number of young members, the church began a choir scholarship program for college students, hoping to build intentional bridges of welcome for single people. Now, when a person in her twenties walks into the sanctuary, she sees a half a dozen people like herself, up front, participating in worship leadership.

Organic Growth

In my churches' experience, the intentional process of making space for intergenerational connections to flourish often eventuates in wonderful surprises. We never know exactly where or how the development will take place. The church becomes a strange kind of farmer, like the ones in Jesus's parables, tending soil, getting rid of rocks, pulling weeds, and planting seeds. With a great deal of prayer, hope, and planning, we prepare the soil, but we don't know how growth actually happens, and rich beautiful flowers can bloom in the strangest places.

We learned how intergenerational communities grew up in our church in Barrington, Rhode Island. We were on the main road of a scenic New England town and the bookends that held the street together were landmark historic churches: the red church and the white church. Mothers drove by those lovely structures and dreamed about having their daughters' weddings there. They barely glanced at our sanctuary on the other side of the street. We did not have gentle white slats or historic brick; we had a simple concrete block sanctuary tucked back from that main road.

The congregation began an intentional process of building intergenerational connections, and I wanted to get a sense of where the membership had some energy and passion, so we met in small groups and talked about our hopes and plans for the next few years.

In each group, landscaping came up as a top priority. I breathed deeply and shook my head each time this came up, because in my mind, it should have been the last of our priorities. Yet, when we developed our long-term strategy, I placed it on the top of our list, given the congregation's stated interest.

Our church was constructed in a U shape, the buildings wrapped around a neglected patch of land with an assortment of overgrown grasses and bubbling asphalt. One day, a group of us gathered and planned a beautiful oriental garden, with a bent pine, delicate white flowers, granite benches, and flagstone paths. It was going to take a great deal of money for our little church to create this garden, and I did not know how it would be possible. But we began, trimming back the tree, picking out the flagstone and the granite benches. During Easter and anniversary celebrations, the children gathered to plant bulbs in the space. Gradually, the garden became a reality. Money came in through a large memorial gift; a variety of generous people started contributing hours of backbreaking labor, and we began to see those sketchy plans grow and bloom.

Just like the parables Jesus told, the seeds of labor began to spring up to create a deep spiritual connection within the church. An Alcoholics Anonymous group that met in our fellowship hall gave us a note, thanking us for this important meditation garden. It had become a place for people to walk and take the steps of sobriety.

I noticed a woman in her early sixties, who had just lost her husband to a hungry cancer, stepping around the stones in silent reflection before her loved one's funeral.

The garden quickly spread, cherry trees were planted in the front lawn and people began tirelessly working, pulling out the invasive poison ivy and prickly red berries that had grown up. Two wonderful women, Gail and Deb, joined the church and jumped in, finding a place of service within the congregation. On Saturday and Sunday afternoons, they pulled on their work boots and cleared out the unwanted shrubs and leaves.

Gail and Deb cultivated another spot around the side of the church that they named the "Anything Goes, Everything Grows" garden. People brought the particularly beautiful cuttings from their own yards and placed them in the fertile soil. One person who felt alienated from the congregation timidly planted some flowers from his yard, and Deb quickly affirmed his gift to garden, giving him the validation that he needed from the community.

In the midst of all of this, Anna arrived. She was in her late thirties, athletic, and tall. One Sunday morning, she cycled by the church and noticed the new life springing up. The gardens lured her, she got off of her bike, wandered into the back row of the sanctuary after the service started, and left the moment the last hymn was sung. She returned each Sunday that followed, so I began to chase her down, trying to make some sort of connection, while trying to respect her obvious desire to remain anonymous.

Then one morning, Anna stopped by my office on one of her bike rides. This thin, robust woman—a picture of health—sat in the chair across from me and told me that she was riddled with cancer. It was stage four and she didn't have more than a few months to live. Anna had not been to church since she was a child, but when she saw the flowers springing up, she was somehow drawn to our sanctuary. She asked me if I could teach her how to pray.

We began trading books, I prayed for her, and she learned how to pray. She didn't want the congregation to know about her condition; she seemed unwilling to make too many new friends. She just needed a space in that important time. In her final months, she longed to nurture her connection with God and I watched as her bond grew deep and rich as the gardens around our sanctuary matured and expanded.

Then one Sunday, Anna no longer showed up. When I called her home, there was no answer. I hung up the receiver and sat at my desk for a moment. Then, spontaneously, I walked out to the garden. With nervous energy, I circled the flowers over and over again, letting the reality of her death settle within me. When I rested on the cold granite bench, gratitude began to flourish as well; I was so grateful for the time I had had with her, and I knew that within our worshiping community Anna had learned to nurture her bond with God. Through the church, and through those gardens, Anna found her spiritual home and realized her calling to die well.

Months before when we listed "landscaping" as a goal in our long-term planning process, I had no idea what kind of rich intergenerational connection would grow up with those iris bulbs. As the oldest man planned the garden, the youngest toddlers planted flowers, and everybody in between hauled asphalt, spread mulch, and laid paths, the miraculous thing was how God worked through this creation. During that precious process of renewal, our bonds with each other strengthened and we watched the Holy Spirit blossom with those flowers.

Reflection Questions

1. We can begin by thinking about adults in terms of generations, in our congregations and our society. On a board, write down five headings:

20-30	31-40	41-50	51–70	71+

Under each section, list the things that people in each age group are going through. What sort of challenges are they facing? What events in their lifetime formed how they think? What political and economic forces shaped their generation? What were the general religious currents with which they grew up? What sorts of attributes and characteristics would you use to describe your own age group?

2. Send out spies. Just like Moses sent out spies to check out the Promised Land, you can send out different people to assess the particular areas of your church. Look particularly to see if the space is pleasant, clean, child-friendly, and well marked. How would you rate the following spaces: entrance, sanctuary, education rooms, nursery, and offices?

What sort of things could be improved, so that each generation might feel welcome? Is the entrance easy to find from the parking lot? Are there children's bulletins, or something for them to draw on during worship? What does the artwork in the education rooms look like? Are there step stools in the bathroom and at the water fountains? How do the toys in the nursery look?

CHAPTER 3

Encouraging Economic Understanding

A friend recently went to an ATM near his Chicago apartment building to withdraw some cash, and the machine spewed out a little white paper with a negative number on his balance. "What is *wrong* with me?" he berated himself. "I'm thirty-five years old and in the red. How can that be possible? Am I just a moron or what?"

Of course he's not a moron; he's an extremely responsible grown adult, living with the debts of an expensive education in a high rent city on a stagnant salary. He's just like the rest of the twenty- and thirty-year-olds in our country, at least those who did not go into certain areas of law or business. And my friend is a part of a vast number of people who hate themselves because of their economic situation.

As congregations reach out to include younger adults in their spiritual communities, they do well to understand that younger generations find themselves struggling in an enormous economic crisis not of their own making. To climb into the middle class, people in their twenties and thirties often live under a towering mountain of interest payments, and most people in younger generations do not make any decisions without first consulting their debt load. The economic predicament that younger generations endure affects their career choices, living arrangements, family structures, quality of life, church commitments, and ability to have children.

With accessible credit, the face of poverty has changed. Many of the young families who get dressed up for church on Sunday morning, who have children in smart pants and flowery dresses, who smile and shake the pastor's hand on the way out of the service, who live in houses in good neighborhoods with neatly trimmed lawns, many of these families are trying to figure out how they are going to buy groceries this week or they are meeting with a lawyer on Monday to discuss the details of bankruptcy laws.

After attending good colleges and working hard every day, young families struggle under tremendous educational debt and jumbo mortgages. With two necessary incomes supporting families it only takes an unexpected illness, a child who needs additional care, or a layoff to shatter the delicate economic foundation supporting young households.[1]

"What's Wrong with Us?"

Of course, this picture of economic instability among young adults can be confusing. When we look at families, we often see two incomes, SUVs, expensive video games, and houses that cost ten times what a house cost in the seventies. Every son is a soccer star and every daughter is a princess. The church and society is pervaded by the myth that a two-profession household allows one to live in luxury. Young adults often think that everyone else is living the good life, spending their free time day trading and watching their Microsoft stock catapult through the roof of their McMansions.

Some people in their twenties and thirties are doing well, but the vast majority struggle. In my tribe, we spend lovely evenings eating at home by candlelight, gathered around our mismatched dining room sets, bragging to each other about our latest thrift store finds. We discuss the distressing advice that our parents thoughtfully tell us, especially their admonition to spend less than 20 percent of our income on a mortgage, but we are painfully aware that we simply cannot find houses that cheap or salaries that high (even with two adults working). We know how we live, but we have this gnawing suspicion that everyone else is smart, disciplined, and rich, and it's that which leads us to ask, "What's wrong with us?"

This self-repulsion exists for many reasons, but as a pastor, I am most concerned with two simultaneous factors: (1) we live with a cultural and religious attitude that equates economic instability with moral failure, and (2) people under forty struggle financially.

Economic Instability and Morality

Since Max Weber, we have linked capitalism, Protestantism, and wealth into a cycle as sure as collection, evaporation, and precipitation. We believe that morality is linked with discipline, and discipline is connected with wealth. Yet with this focus on the tree, we lose sight of the complicated forest. When the pine does not thrive in the drought of the wilderness, we blame the pine. Linguist and activist George Lakoff contends that our country's myth that a person can pull herself up by her bootstraps and overcome any circumstance disregards our larger economic landscape and it can also lead us to think that a poor person is not disciplined and is, therefore, immoral.[2]

Mary Pipher, an author and psychologist with a private practice in Lincoln, Nebraska, also notices this unfortunate connection between wealth and morality when she describes the ethos of younger generations, "Money confers moral superiority and poverty is considered a moral crime, a sign of personal failure."[3]

This link seems most apparent when churches look for pastoral leadership. In seminary, I was warned that it's now commonplace for search committees to secretly pull up a credit report on prospective pastors. Looking at their scores, they search for qualities of a responsible and honest person, so they scrutinize our monthly payments without any background information.

Having myself worked in finance, this practice makes me shudder. After all, a great many mistakes exist on those reports. People are regularly victimized by identity theft, mortgage companies err, and sometimes (heaven forbid) a person might even misplace a bill. When I went through reports with my customers to find out the explanations behind their scores, I often heard credible stories of family death or hospitalization. But the church does not allow a prospective pastor this courtesy. The relentless and unforgiving world of credit reporting has seeped into our pastoral search committees, who might conclude that if the candidate's credit score is low, then she is immoral and unfit for the pastorate.

The link between morality and economic stability looks different, depending on the culture of the congregation. I grew up in the 1980s when a "prosperity gospel" was preached on a regular basis at my conservative church. The promise of riches extended from God to Abraham to the rest of us, or so we were told, and it was God's plan that we would become a part of this Abrahamic Covenant: we were to be rich. Religious leaders regularly told me that the United States was a *wealthy* nation because it was a *Christian* nation.

It would seem that this message would have alienated middle- and lower-class people, but it didn't. In part, this may have been an outcome of our mission practices. When conservatives engaged in helping the needy, they often saw it as an opportunity for evangelizing. They were concerned with feeding the soul as well as the body, and they actively persuaded the poor to become a part of their religious communities. It followed that many conservative churches had regular social contact with people in lower classes; they worshiped with the people they fed. In fact, in one church that I attended as a teenager, half of the sanctuary space was lined with canned food so that the poor people worshiping there could pick up the groceries they needed for the week.

Now, with the highly political nature of current conservative churches, the idea remains that with morality comes discipline, and with discipline comes wealth. Yet, when this is preached to a spectrum of classes, it can be less of a condemnation and more of a hopeful message. Conservative churches do not shy away from giving financial advice to their members. That prosperity gospel message of my youth also came with harsh warnings against credit card use and junior high Sunday school lessons on compounded interest.

In mainline churches, the overt message toward the poor is different, but may be even more discouraging because the middle and lower classes often steer clear of the denominational labels.[4] Progressives have an entirely dissimilar mission practice, as we see feeding the body as an act of hospitality. We give aid because we love our neighbor as we love ourselves, because each person is made in the image of God and is a person of dignity, because we are trying to be servants of God. We maintain that proselytizing the needy in conjunction with helping them can lead to the cruel manipulation of vulnerable populations. We would never ask anyone to listen to a sermon or recite a prayer before they could get a shower and a hot meal.

The understandable outcome is that the poor we help rarely become the poor alongside whom we worship. We are used to working with the poverty "out there," but sometimes our only real contact is the benevolence check that we write. By the time a person walks into the door of a mainline church, he usually has his financial portfolio in pretty good order.

Another awkward truth is that some members of mainline churches can show subtle but harsh intolerance toward middle and lower classes. I joined the Presbyterian Church in my early twenties while I was employed in a retail position, and as I look back and recall the raised eyebrows, I'm surprised that I stayed. If it weren't for the supportive care of my wonderful pastor, I'm sure the front entry on that prestigious downtown church would have become a revolving door, spitting me out as fast as I'd come in.

While working at a cash register at a seminary bookstore as a divinity student, I became appalled at how my soon-to-be colleagues treated me. At the end of the day, I was never quite sure if I really wanted to join the club.

My discomfort over the prejudice compounded as the years progressed. I once overheard a conversation in the fellowship hall of a church located in an affluent suburb of New York City. Over cookies and coffee, one member was telling another about a visitor. "She's a lawyer," she announced, and both heads bobbed agreeably.

"What school did she attend?" he asked.

A concerned look darkened the woman's face as she mumbled the name of the institution.

"Hmmm," he faltered. "That's not very impressive."

She agreed, with a deep sigh and a mournful sip of coffee.

I have learned, after some embarrassing experiences, to be careful taking minister colleagues to a restaurant where I am friends with one of the wait staff, because I'm afraid I'll leave in shame at how the employee was treated. Somehow the mainline church's healthy passion for education can become a boorish disdain for those who never attended college, or for those who have a PhD and yet find themselves waiting tables.

These notions drown out Jesus, standing on the Mount, telling us that the poor are blessed. Instead, we have the idea that anyone who does not make it into the upper-middle class is undisciplined, vaguely immoral, and needs to put in some more hours to make ends meet. We see poverty as an issue of personal responsibility, not a systemic problem, and if a person is struggling, then it is she who must be bad or lazy, not the social system. There must be an easy solution to the problem, we think. If only she'd cut back on the lattes or quit spending so much with her credit cards. She needs to look at her budget and stop thinking about the iPod. She just needs to work a little harder—like the rest of us.

Economic Landscape of Younger Generations

Although cost-cutting measures can be helpful, the solution to economic hardship is not usually simple.[5] Most young adults struggle. The economic landscape of our society has changed dramatically and is made up of countless valleys and very few mountains, so the possibility of moving up has become unobtainable for many in my generation. There are much larger problems for young people in the middle class that won't be solved no matter how much frugality they exercise. Rising educational debts, high mortgages, and low wages converge upon people in their twenties and thirties so that they are two miles underground before they even begin their climb up the corporate ladder.[6]

It's a confusing picture because I rarely open the newspaper without reading a story about some young family spending a fortune on granite kitchen counters or how our country drains away as much money on bathroom remodeling as the GNP of many developing countries.[7] Of course, just as we can't judge how all twenty-year-olds live through the example of Paris Hilton, neither can we always understand the economic situation of people under forty by what we observe in the Style pages of our paper.

The other confounding thing is that if you are over forty, it may seem like you are wandering in the same forest as someone in his twenties or thirties. But you are not. I often hear, "What's the big deal? I was poor when I was young. We all were. We want everything that our parents have right away, but we have to wait for it. That's just the way it is." Well, things have changed for those born after 1970, and it's not due to our sense of entitlement, spending practices, or working habits.[8]

In 2000, the median net worth of someone over sixty-five was twice the worth of all households, and *fifteen times* the net worth of households headed by those under thirty-five.[9] In that same year, the rate of home ownership for people who were 65 to 74 years old was 81.3 percent, the highest home ownership rate ever in this country. For those under 25, the rate was only 20 percent. The percentage spread between the 65 and the 25 year olds was the largest since 1960.[10]

It's no secret that the rich have been getting richer and the poor poorer in this country, but with the combination of the rising cost of college, skyrocketing real estate, and stagnant salaries, we are creating an entire generation that could be doomed to poverty.[11] Plus, shifts in employment practices have made a huge difference for people entering the work force in the new millennium.

Employment

Many people who enter the labor force go into retail, like my husband and I did after four years of college. While General Motors used to be the country's largest employer, Wal-Mart is now the largest. And while those union jobs at GM in 1970 used to provide $17.50 an hour, now most people work at Wal-Mart for $8 an hour.[12]

Of course, beginning in retail is not a terrible thing. In fact, it's something we've always done in our country. My father often tells me stories about his employment as a butcher in his parents' grocery store and my mom tells about working in her parents' ice cream shop. They were, no doubt, being paid a very low wage, if any wage at all. Yet they were contributing to their families' wealth, which eventually sent them to college and secretarial school. Plus, they were learning many valuable things about owning and running a business as their parents mentored them by working alongside them.

In this current retail structure, however, the low wages are not made up by accumulated family wealth; in fact, the affluence of the store is rarely even seen in the community-at-large. Many times, after years of profitable business, a company moves from the town and leaves nothing but a giant concrete shell and a parking lot where paradise used to be. And the pyramid that may have provided young workers some mentoring and upward mobility is obsolete, as managers are replaced by "team leaders" who get a fifty-cent raise for their supervisory job. The jobs have been stripped down to bare and mindless tasks, with all the major decisions coming out of a central office. The responsibility, challenge, and creativity have been taken out of the positions, so employees don't learn any skills for further advancement.

Businesses now outsource a great deal of work so that they don't have to pay benefits like health insurance and so that they can easily adapt to a changing market by taking on employees or (more typically) downsizing by getting rid of their temporary workers. With young people making up half of our temporary labor force, often as freelancers and consultants, the number of uninsured Americans keeps rising.[13] In 2006, 46.6 million people had no insurance coverage.[14] Thirty percent of those aged between 19 and 29 do not have health insurance.[15] That's more than any other age group.

Most of my friends have yet to find their lives settled. Many of them are not happy with their jobs, particularly if they work as temps or without benefits. Typically they either live in urban areas where the rent is way above their means or they have to pick up and move every couple of years. They spend a lot of their time on the phone assessing and reassessing the situation, wondering if they will ever be able to own a home, if they will ever find their soul mate, if they will ever have any financial stability, or if they will ever be able to afford to have children.

People in their twenties and thirties are in difficult situations. Knowing that they will never accumulate the wealth that their parents have, they wonder if they'll ever be able to pay off their school bills. They begin saving (or at least are told they should) for their children's college educations before they are even born, and they are aware that Social Security will probably not be around in the same way when they turn sixty-five, so they know they need to save more for retirement, if they ever have that luxury.

Young adults have taken to heart the advice to work harder. Now that this generation of "slackers" has entered the workforce, people work longer hours than any other industrialized country.[16] And while, the productivity, or the amount that an average worker produces in an hour, has risen steadily, the median hourly wage for workers has declined.[17]

The economic frustrations magnify when these young adults are constantly, consistently told that their instability is their own fault. When I spoke to a college student in Texas about student loans, she repeated the same line I often hear, "Students now, we just spend way too much money. My parents worked hard and were frugal. They didn't expect so much. That's why they're in such a better position than I am."

We talked a bit more, and I found out that her parents had in fact worked as students, making enough money to pay for their rent *and* their tuition—an impossible feat for a student today. Most students work, but their incomes barely cover the electricity bill; they could never come close to paying off their tuitions during their school years.

Financial stress affects people in their twenties and thirties in different ways and much of it depends on if a person is single or married, male or female, a parent or childless.

SINGLE OR MARRIED

Single people often move to urban areas for career opportunities, but then they find themselves priced out of the housing market. The median rents in urban areas rose more than 50 percent from 1995 to 2002, and now young adults can expect to spend more than 22 percent of their income on rent.[18] To further frustrate matters, landlords often refuse to rent to single people. And these same single people face discrimination when it comes to insurance rates, taxes, passing on inheritances, and parental laws. [19]

Single people who want to marry typically put off commitments until they are "financially stable." This used to mean that a young man might wait a year after college so that he could get an established job and buy a home before popping the question. Now it's much different, as financial security and home ownership can rarely be achieved on one income. Establishing an independent household can be much more difficult now. Among adults aged 18 to 24, 57 percent of men and 47 percent of women still live with their parents. Among those between the ages of 25 and 34, 13 percent of men and 8 percent of women live at home.[20]

When young adults predict their futures together, planning out their professional lives can be a complicated chess match: as one moves, the other also tries to move forward, but he can only strategize as long as a space becomes available.

That same young man, living in the twenty-first century, finds himself caught in a vicious cycle. He puts off familial obligations until he can find a steady job with benefits, but those jobs are rare. Then, as he begins to look for real estate, he cannot afford the mortgage on one salary. So, young couples often live together before they're married, because it takes two salaries to attain that sought-after stability or even just to make ends meet.[21]

In the highly-charged political atmosphere of Washington, we often hear about things that are a threat to the institution of marriage, but we rarely hear how our economy affects it. A lack of money and insurance can cause havoc in a relationship and it can certainly stall anticipated nuptials.

To Be or Not to Be Parents

The average age of a woman when she has her first child has risen significantly in the last thirty years.[22] For women who have children, a lot of ground has been gained, as more women enroll in college and more job opportunities are available to mothers, but we have a long way to go. Traditionally, as people begin their careers they tend to sacrifice a bit in their twenties and thirties to establish themselves and move up the ladder. This becomes complicated for young women because this upward movement needs to happen at the same time that they are most suited to having children. Women may become less flexible at a time when they need to be the most mobile.

Our workplaces are far from family-friendly, and decades after the feminist revolution, women still make 78 cents to every dollar that a man makes. At the end of a lifetime of work, those 22 cents add up to one million dollars.[23] Families need this difference. A woman's salary is no longer the "additional income," but the necessary income.

Our answer to this crisis shows a failure in the feminist imagination as women spill endless ink over the mommy wars. Often fueled by religious institutions, women who work at home criticize women who earn a paycheck as bad moms who neglect their children and abandon their priorities. Women who are paid for their work point fingers at moms at home, calling them fanatics, saying they're selling themselves short as their expensive educations go to waste because of their choices. Most women feel caught in the middle of this tug-of-war, feeling tremendous guilt both over staying at home *and* going to work.

This upper-middle-class war neglects the reality of most parents. Most of them do not have a choice any longer: they have to work for pay.[24] Yet churches often lead the battle cry to make sure that women care for their children by staying home with them, and it's unusual to find spiritual communities who speak out for working women or advocate for them.

So our women's circles and Bible studies happen at 10:00 a.m. on weekday mornings, or right around supper and bedtime on a Wednesday night, both times when most young women can't attend. Our church functions often do not provide for children, leaving mothers out as well. There is constant murmuring in some churches that our customs are dying because this new generation of mothers is not picking up the work load—as if every mom should come home from a fifty-hour work week, clean the house, cook the meals, do the laundry, send the children off to bed, and then go to a two-hour church meeting to run a bake sale. Unfortunately, at the end of all of this, mothers can feel disconnected with their worshiping communities, and they are left with the notion that churches do not support them.

To further the frustration of parents who struggle financially, the attitude that "poor people are bad" is highly concentrated in the world of parenting. We want the very best for our children, and though our sacrifices are admirable, they can lead to a worrisome trend of buying good parenting.

Karen realized this when she went to a playgroup that was set up in the fellowship hall of her neighborhood Methodist Church. She worked as a counselor while her husband held temporary jobs and stayed home so that he could take care of their toddler. They were financially stretched, lived without cable television, a cell phone, or Internet service, and traded off their one used car, but they considered themselves lucky because one parent could be home and work at the same time.

Karen's child played with the others, setting up blocks and cradling baby dolls, while the moms sat along the edge of the hall talking about the best pediatrician, the best school, the best dentist.

"What preschool does your child attend?" One mom asked Karen.

Karen flushed a bit and answered, "My daughter doesn't go to preschool. She's only two." The truth was that Karen had looked into preschools in the area, but their tuition rivaled the cost of a state university. There was no way that she could afford it.

"Well, then your child should be in pre-preschool."

Karen smiled, "What exactly does a kid learn in pre-preschool?"

The mom was quick in her defense, "It's absolutely essential for a child's development to be in a structured environment for those formative years. My son learns to sit in a circle, follow directions, all kinds of things. It's been proven over and over: early childhood education is a top priority for getting your daughter into the Ivy Leagues."

Karen avoided eye contact with the adamant and precociously ambitious mom. "Well, I guess we're going to be home-schooling our daughter's pre-preschooling."

It seemed that Karen and her husband lived through that excruciating conversation at least once a week. Even when they simply admitted they didn't have the money to send their child to preschool, people were still determined that they should somehow *find* the money for their child's education.

"Somewhere along the way, I guess the rules changed," Karen confided in aggravation. "Now we're supposed to have one parent home *and* be able to put our child in preschool. People act as if we're abusing our child because we live in a neighborhood with poorly performing schools, but it's the only house we could afford. The worst part about it is that the pressure is so intense that I feel like a bad mom at the end of these conversations—just because we don't make enough money."

Doing the "right thing" for our children often means taking on a mortgage that we can barely afford so we can move into a better neighborhood with good school systems, or taking out interest-only mortgages to pay for private schooling. Even with a child in public school, the financial strain can be a burden. In my daughter's elementary school, the Parent Teacher Association holds over 50 fundraisers a year to fortify our child's education.

But the pressures of providing for our children's educations are not where it ends. Juliet Schor's book *Born to Buy* reveals just how fiercely our culture markets to children. Even when parents limit television viewing, children are targeted in almost every public space in their lives: classrooms, museums, menus, and restrooms.[25] Through Schor's meticulous data, she proves that this concentrated consumer culture contributes to a rise in anxiety and depression for kids.[26]

The stress on parents intensifies as bankruptcies erupt among middle-class families. Now, as economists Elizabeth Warren and Amelia Warren Tyagi write, the difference between becoming broke or remaining solvent depends on whether you have children or not.[27]

From Generation to Generation

The intergenerational aspects of our economy make the landscape even more interesting. In 2002, I attended a fiscal responsibility seminar sponsored by the Presbyterian Church's Board of Pensions. Gathered in a seminary classroom with a group of other pastors, the facilitator was driving home the problem of high-interest credit cards and loans. The discussion reminded me of a couple of friends from the West Coast whose twelve-year-old car broke down for the last time. With their third child on the way, they needed to buy a used minivan so that all of the car seats could be securely fastened—an impossible feat in a regular car. Because a mistake (on the mortgage company's part) showed up on their credit report, the bank charged them 21 percent interest for the auto loan.

I raised my hand, explained the situation and wondered out loud why the wealthy grandparents did not loan them the money instead.

After all, the grandparents had their money in a bank, where the bank was using it to make a decent profit. The same bank was lending money to the parents, and making a killing. So why not do something to stop the bank's immoral practice of predatory lending?[28] Why not strive for economic justice within the family by cutting out the outrageously expensive middleman? The grandparents could lend the money to the parents, and charge the same amount of interest that they were getting from their CDs. It was a logical solution; instead of a struggling couple with three children paying $22,300 for a $15,000 van, they could borrow from the grandparents at a six percent rate and save $5,300. Why should the bank make all that money at both families' expense? It would be a very unwise stewardship practice. After all, the loan would make just a small dent in the parent's CDs.

I suddenly found myself in the midst of an intense intergenerational skirmish. The majority of ministers around me, who were closing in on their retirement, were furious that I would suggest such a thing. The argument continued and heated up to a fever pitch. The facilitator refused to weigh in on either side and finally told us to take it outside during the break.

The parents did not wait for me to step outside. The second a break was called, they surrounded my desk, arguing some more. Yet, without the large audience, their demeanor changed, and I saw frustrated moms and dads who wanted to make sure that their retirement was secure and felt torn about not supporting their struggling sons and daughters more. "After all," one woman admitted, "my parents helped us in rough times. They gave us the down payment for our house after we got out of seminary."

"Yes, that's true for me too," a man admitted, but not wanting to give up any ground, he added, "but my parents didn't have so many years of retirement to worry about." He wanted to make sure that he had enough money to not be a burden on his sons and daughters in the years to come. The parents were afraid that if they started lending money to their adult offspring, then they would not be able to turn off the fountain of mercy. They feared that they would end up forgiving their debtors, and losing their independence in retirement. Plus they had a deeper concern for their sons and daughters: they worried about fostering unhealthy dependence with their monetary support. They were anxious that writing a check would discourage their children from becoming full members of society.

I didn't realize that with my innocent conclusion I was entering into a national debate with desperate feelings on both sides. Now I have become more aware of this tension in our country: parents raised their children to be autonomous and independent, yet many of them have exhibited a "failure to launch." Movies, hotel commercials, newspapers, and magazine articles portray a loser son, living in the basement of his parent's apartment, feeling entitled to everything, but not willing to work for anything.

When I recall the concern on my colleagues' faces, I still think that family members should alleviate the pressure on young adults by deterring rapacious lending, if they can do it without jeopardizing their own finances.

Of course, a lot of working people under forty would never ask their parents for help. When a young adult has a looming car repair or medical treatment that will cost thousands of dollars, it's much easier to pick up the credit card than to pick up the phone and ask mom or dad. In their mailboxes, they have six letters a day, in every form and size, with companies begging them to borrow money from them. Why would they ask their parents for money, humiliating themselves and looking like losers? Yet a person's livelihood can easily become buried in unending interest if the credit card is his only option.

On the other hand, the concern for people entering retirement is a solid fear. Close to a third of retiring people have no assets saved.[29] With the rising cost of health care, millions of people will live far longer than their assets can support them. In our own families, older generations will not be looking for individual solutions based on complete self-reliance. We will be supporting each other.

Lynn realized this. She raised her daughters to be independent: she felt that financial and emotional autonomy would be their highest achievement as adults. Then she spent a weekend taking care of her sick mom, who couldn't afford good nursing care at the end of her life. As Lynn transferred her mother from the wheelchair to the toilet bowl, it struck her how fleeting self-sufficiency is.

Even though Lynn has money saved for her retirement, she knows that she will inevitably be dependent on her daughters. She told me,

"You know, it just hit me. I realized they will be doing that for me someday, so if they need help from me now, that's okay."

A few small solutions might be found within our families, but certainly not most of them. We need a comprehensive approach. It will be vital for us to transfer this problem into the public arena. This situation is not because of the irresponsible failure of one son or one daughter. Just as one tree's vitality depends on the entire forest, our economic situation is a larger problem that stems from high mortgages, increased student loans, and stagnant wages. It is aggravated by predatory lending practices, temporary employment, the absence of health insurance, and the lack of support for fragile two-income families.

When looking at generational issues, we can have some economic consideration for young adults. We can stop thinking of young people as purely materialistic and irresponsible, and begin understanding their larger financial situation. We can begin thinking about social justice for young adults, which includes requiring responsible lending by banks, increasing gutted government assistance for education, and pressuring corporations to boost wages and benefits. We can look for ways to medically insure all Americans, especially the children and young adults who are most affected by the cuts in coverage. These may seem like unobtainable goals for the local church, but our country has seen faith communities take up much larger challenges than these, with great results. Finally, we can begin to attend to the spiritual issues that arise from the fear and anxiety that these financial issues cause.

A Spiritual Problem

When ministering to people in their twenties and thirties, church leaders do well to understand that economic struggles have a tremendous impact on people under forty. Many people in my generation are consumed with the stress and anxiety of their financial situation, as Anya Kamenetz writes,

> Generation Debt's sea of trouble isn't just economic or political. It approaches the spiritual. We are restless as well as strapped. The common thread joining all members of this generation is a sense of

permanent impermanence. It's hard to commit to a family, a community, a job, or a life path when you don't know if you'll be able to make a living, make a marriage last, or live free of debt.[30]

The net result of this economic crisis is a spiritual crisis. Although we have typically not talked about it, churches must begin to understand the financial situation of adults under forty. Economic instability is something that can keep young adults awake at night. It keeps them from ever feeling like they can make commitments. It can consume their lives with worry and tension.

Our spiritual communities should not assume that each young person who struggles is just not responsible or not disciplined or not smart enough to make it. We can begin by rethinking our theology surrounding money, class, and God's blessings. As religious institutions we can take a stand and support instead of insulting working mothers, and begin to look for meaningful ways to encourage parents in our communities.

Permanent Renters

My husband and I bought the house that we were renting last April. Actually, we bought two-thirds of our house; Western Presbyterian owns one-third of it, through a shared equity arrangement. We signed the papers on a wet spring day, and though our closing was complete with all the typical anxiety-inducing, last-minute frustrations, we came home feeling giddy and relieved.

As the sun set in our neighborhood, we did not waste any time trimming back shrubs, fertilizing the flowers, and generally putting energy into the house that we had not put into it when we rented. We were responsible renters, but our commitment was limited. We paid what was due each month and called the owners if anything went wrong. We kept things properly maintained, but made minimal investments in improving the property.

That changed when we took out the mortgage. Suddenly, the joys and responsibilities of home ownership became ours, and with our newly acquired assets and debts, we became more a part of a community. Relationships could form because we were on a different level of commitment. The people who live across the street from us came out and began talking to us, welcoming us to the neighborhood, even though we had already lived there for eight months.

As the sun began to set, I took one last look at my new community and smiled. I wiped my feet as I stepped inside the house, thinking about how strange it was that ownership made us so much more a part of things. It was not just our neighbors who hesitated forging a relationship while we were renters, it was also me. In that temporary state, I did not want to make connections that would quickly sever when our lease was up. Yet, as the owner of the property, things were different. I could breathe deeper, knowing that there was permanence in my position. My child would soon be attending kindergarten at the public school. I would begin to follow local politics and join the neighborhood association.

Many young adults in our current economic situation have not had the possibility of owning anything; they've become permanent renters. They have no ability to become a stable part of a community. They cannot afford to sign more than a year's lease because their futures are so uncertain. After all, when layoffs occur in a company, they affect young employees the most.[31]

A good friend and vice-president of a large company reminds me that a person should expect to get laid off at least once in his or her career. The loyalty that bound employers and employees has been eroded so younger generations have learned to watch very carefully for the writing on the wall and remain ready for a shift in vocation at any time. That adaptability often means short-term living arrangements and long geographical moves.

With this tenuous situation, people under forty are not only renters, but they are also rented. As temporary workers, companies buy their time without any commitments. With no insurance to take care of their physical needs, no assurance that gainful employment will be available for more than a short stint, and no corporate investment in their professional formation, young adults lose a sense of relationship, connection, and stability. The economic environment breeds a system where young adults are not seen as people but as productive units that can be disposed of quickly and painlessly when the contract runs out.

With the average length of a job lasting 2.7 years, young adults have difficulty making pledges to our neighborhoods, churches, friends, and partners. Our real economic situation greatly affects our spiritual economy. We have difficulty giving and receiving in our tenuous positions.

Economics of Spiritual Community

During stewardship time, when we plan how to encourage giving in our congregations, I often hear, "We are the most prosperous nation to ever live. We've got to teach these young people how to give."

As a person in her thirties, I wonder how this claim of prosperity holds up for my generation. Can we be counted as part of this prosperity when our debts so heavily outweigh our assets? We have lovely commodities available to us, but many young adults do not actually own much. We are so busy paying off the interest that we rarely get to the principle.

We may need to learn how to give, but there's something even more basic than that. Some people in their twenties and thirties need to learn how to be a part of a supportive spiritual economy. We do not know much about an ecosystem in which we can thrive, where our bodies are cared for and nurtured. We have difficulty giving and receiving.

When I think of the situation of young adults today, it reminds me of Peter, in the upper room, refusing the service of Jesus.

Jesus and the disciples are gathered. They've been pretty nomadic themselves, but in the gospel of John, at this moment, they're not traveling, walking, teaching, or healing. They are not going out, they are coming in, and we get a rare picture of what happens when they're all together in one place.

Jesus meets with his friends in an attic room. When he gathers with them, he takes this towel, and he begins to wash their feet. It's usually the job of a servant, and yet their teacher and friend, this man who could not enter into a town without drawing a huge crowd, took a basin of water, got on his knees, and began to wash their dirty feet.

Jesus is in his thirties. There's great emotion in that room: the thrill ferments with a bit of treachery. They had had a really wonderful week with Jesus coming into Jerusalem with immense fan-fare and everyone's expecting him to become a great political leader. The friends relax and drink in the exhilaration of their success. But Jesus (as U2 sings) keeps "talking about the end of the world." Jesus has a sense that he's about to be executed, and at the pinnacle of his popularity and power, he decides to get down on his knees and start washing feet. When Jesus gets to Peter, Peter looks down at Jesus, kneeling there before him, and tells Jesus no. He can't bear to have Jesus doing the work of a servant.

Yet Jesus says that he has to do it, or Peter will have no part of him. So Peter gives it up, and he lets Jesus wash his feet.

I understand Peter. There's something very modern about Peter's sensibilities when he doesn't want Jesus to serve him. It's hard to let people help, when we're expected to be so autonomous and all together, and we know that we're not. It is difficult to receive an outstretched hand, an arm of mercy. Many young adults long for support, but don't know how to receive it.

This is the thing: we don't want to be in a place where we owe one more person. It's that strange economy. You do me a favor, and I reply, "I owe you one." It's more than just an expression, there's some truth to it. And the truth is a burden.

When Jesus takes Peter's foot in his hands, pours the water over his dusty toes, makes sure that the mud is no longer sticking to his soles, when Jesus pats Peter's feet dry with his towel, in this great act of servitude and friendship, Peter is given a part of Jesus. Peter owes Jesus something.

And such is the nature of friendship, giving, and spiritual com-munity. We become a part of one another; we carry a bit of one another with us. We learn to give and to receive, not as simple commodities, as people buying and selling hours, but as complicated bodies with abundance and necessities. We build community with one another, with all of our assets and all of our needs, taking into consideration the requirements of our hands, hearts, and feet.

We give as we are able, and often we must learn to receive. For a generation that is consistently characterized as entitled, covetous slack-ers, receiving from others can make us very uncomfortable. None of us likes to be in debt, especially when we are tired of owing so much, but that's the nature of spiritual community.

So it is that in our churches, when tribes begin to form, we must understand the tenuous financial position of many young adults. If we ignore their economic landscape, or quickly dismiss young adults as irresponsible, materialistic, and excessive, we cannot fully understand their context. Yet, if we have consideration for their situation, we will be able to appreciate their reluctance to become active parts of our communities and we will learn ways to minister effectively, creating a healthy spiritual exchange.

Our churches can deftly respond to the settings of young adults by fostering intergenerational connection and encouraging economic understanding. Then we can continue to form tribal communities with unambiguous inclusion, affirming traditions, shared leadership, and spiritual guidance.

Reflection Questions

1. When you were growing up, how did your family talk about money and class? Did you learn anything about these matters from your church? What sort of implicit lessons did you learn about money?

2. How has our attitude toward poverty changed as a nation? How has the church shaped the changes? How has the church responded to them?

3. When considering the economic position of many twenty and thirty year olds, what solutions can you think of that might strengthen the futures of young adults?

4. What is the focus of the campus ministries in your denomination? In what ways are they thinking about economic concerns for their college students?

5. Would a lower- or middle-class person feel comfortable at your church? Would an upper-class person be welcome? What is your church's attitude toward people who do not have a college education?

6. How could your church deepen its understanding of the economic situation of young adults? How can your congregation respond to it?

CHAPTER 4

Cultivating
Unambiguous
Inclusion

When I was in kindergarten, I'd come home from school and sneak in to watch television while my older brother and sister were still in their classes. Mom was often busy around the house, so for a half an hour or so I would stretch out on the dark green shag carpet and become the ruler of my 22-inch universe. I had supreme control of the remote; for a rare thirty minutes in my life, with my thumb on those four shiny buttons, I could watch anything I wanted.

I pressed the tiny orange rectangle and after a loud click, I'd wait for the television to warm up. I'd visit each channel before I got to the Public Broadcasting Station, where Mister Rogers zipped up his blue cardigan, changed his shoes, smiled out from the screen, and with genuine gentleness asked, "Won't you be my neighbor?"

It was a low-tech show, with a plastic-molded neighborhood and papier-mâché puppets that couldn't figure out how to move their mouths. My older siblings would never watch it, but before they came home, visiting the neighborhood engrossed me. The slow pace and kindness of the show soothed me. Mister Rogers reached beyond the ordinary child-appropriate subjects and spoke about divorce, assassinations, war, and a host of difficult things in a mild, matter-of-fact manner.

He kept his spot on PBS for years, and as I got older, I wondered how he continued. The shows that grew up around him fed into a child's boundless energy and short attention span. With colorful animation and graceful puppets, other shows kept kids invigorated and entertained; in contrast, Mister Rogers never seemed deterred by the electric speed of children's entertainment, he just kept methodically zipping up his cardigan, smiling and asking anyone who might be watching, "Won't you be my neighbor?"

Fred Rogers, an ordained Presbyterian minister, did something amazing through that show: he effectively invited an entire generation of children to be his neighbor. He taught them to think of each other as neighbors and modeled peaceful, considerate behavior. In a very concrete way, he demonstrated to a generation that a neighbor is anyone who might be on our path and with this consistent message he had a vital impact on young adults.

Who's My Neighbor?

Jesus taught that all of the law can be summed up in this: "Love God with all your heart, all your soul, and all your mind. Love your neighbor as you love yourself."

Someone in the crowd asked for clarification. He wanted to know exactly who these neighbors were; he needed a list specifying who he was responsible for loving so that he could know who was in and who was out.

In response, Jesus told a story about the Samaritan who acted with kindness to someone who needed help. The Good Samaritan was a neighbor because of what he practiced, not because of where he came from or what he believed. The law of Jesus was a relationship; it did not factor in the object of the action, it only mattered how the subject responded. Therefore, as Christians, we learn that we don't love a certain number of people on our exclusive list of neighbors; we are to be neighbors to anyone we might encounter along our paths.

In contrast, our mainline denominational churches endlessly debate who's on and who's off our lists. In bitter skirmishes we grapple over the validity of different faiths and the inclusion of people with diverse sexual lifestyles. The United Church of Christ's controversial television advertisement summed up the sentiments of many young Christians by showing two intimidating bouncers securing the velvet ropes at the entrance of a church, choosing who could enter the doors. Some older viewers did not understand the poignancy of this ad; they had never stood outside a club, vying for entrance. Perhaps they did not know how it feels to have your opinions, views, and age group overlooked again and again, but it spoke to me, as a thirty-year-old.

The majority of young adults in our country embrace a variety of cultures and religions, and they know that faithful, loving relationships can grow up between two adults of the same sex. They see their duty as spiritual people as being to treat others as they would like to be treated, and that means that they don't tolerate intolerance.

Throughout the exchanges over the doctrine of salvation and acceptable views of sexuality, as our denominations stand with their clipboards, negotiating who is good enough to be on our list, they frequently leave those under forty on the wrong side of the ropes.

When I hear arguments in the church, I am told that the church needs to stand up against the evil of a diverse culture, and not allow the world to taint the pure message of the gospel. Yet, as a part of an age group which welcomes diversity, it feels like the church is fighting against the very richness and difference of my generation, my friends, and me—a richness and difference it perceives as somehow tainted and sinful.

Validity of Different Religions

That difference extends far beyond sexuality, of course. As a fifteen-year-old, I visited Asia on a trip with Teen Missions, International. As a part of an evangelism team, I traveled with thirty other teenagers so that we could convert the people of Hong Kong to Christianity. We performed puppet shows, sang songs, and passed out tracts detailing the way to salvation by repeating a prayer and asking Jesus into your heart.

For a few gray days, we visited China. I looked out the window of the train and saw rows of sunken rice fields, until the landscape changed. Buildings rose up out of the fog, streets criss-crossed my view, and thousands of bikes appeared in the intersections. We stretched our legs, moving out of the train and onto a bus for a few more hours, but the ride was interrupted as we stopped along the alleyways to shop at jade and ivory factories. I stood in the gray concrete buildings, over rickety tables, and watched as hunched artists created intricate carvings from water, stone, and teeth.

As I folded my legs back into the seat of the bus, I resumed my gaze out of the window while a love for the Chinese culture and people grew within me. But instead of increasing my evangelistic fervor (as was intended by the mission organization), it formed a burning question within me: "How could all of these people be going to hell? How can a billion people be eternally damned largely because they were born in China instead of the United States?" My warmth for this country had arisen in a matter of mere days as a visitor. I knew that God was much more loving than me, so how could God send them all to hell—a place where there would be weeping, gnashing of teeth, and burning for all of eternity?

I spoke to people around me about the struggle, and one of the leaders told me, "Carol, when you die, the glory of heaven will be so amazing that you'll understand the full importance of Jesus's sacrifice and you'll no longer have these questions."

With a furrowed brow, I nodded my head in agreement, but my internal conflict continued. After all, I had many years ahead of me and I couldn't wait until I died for my religion to make sense to me. The heart of my beliefs pounded with God's love, and I could not understand that God created all people, God loved all people—and yet God was sending so many of them to eternal suffering because they had not repeated the prayer that was printed (in English) on the back of the tract I held. The longer I traveled through China, the less I could justify such an exclusivist stance. It was not them, the "others," but my own belief system that had to change under the weight of the heartache I experienced.

Though my theology transformed and I have more inner consistency, the struggle has moved outward, into our denominational settings, where some affirm Jesus Christ as the way and insist that this necessarily excludes every other religious path.

Since that experience twenty years ago, the world has been steadily shrinking. With the Internet, the *Times of India* is just as accessible as the *New York Times*. In this exhilarating period of history, we have increased our travel and the accessibility of information. Griffin Gasink, a college student from George Washington University, explained his surroundings: "When you walk into an elevator on campus, you're standing next to the world. You hear all kinds of languages and every sort of ethnicity is riding with you."

With the Immigration and Nationality Act Amendments in the 1960s, Congress eliminated quotas that favored European immigration and made our borders more open to people around the globe.[1] At the dawn of the new millennium, the non-white population of those over 65 was 16 percent, but for those under 25, the non-white population was 39 percent.[2] This has a wonderful effect on our way of life. Now, in the space of one day, our family eats Mexican burritos for breakfast, Thai curry for lunch, and Lebanese chicken for dinner. Our spiritual lives have been enriched as well; I am increasingly influenced by the Buddhist wisdom of Thich Naht Hahn, the Muslim poetry of Rumi, and the Jewish philosophy of Emmanuel Levinas. For people in our twenties and thirties, our closest friends are often as varied as our culture, and these relationships affect the way that we think about God.

In the urban context of Washington, D.C., people enter into relationships and marry across traditional ethnic and religious lines, and families emerge from these loving bonds of respect. In fact, in 2000, 21 percent of our nation's population was foreign-born or first generation. In our sanctuary, we regularly celebrate weddings between Protestants, Catholics, Jews, and Muslims.

Many of us in younger generations don't understand our denominations' wrestling to exclude the legitimacy of other religions; in fact, we thrive on the diversity. Even Jean Twenge, who paints a negative picture of those born after 1970 in her book *Generation Me,* concedes that

In just four decades, the United States has undergone a transformation of attitudes about women, minorities, and gays and lesbians. The revolution of equality was, without question, the largest social change in America in the last half of the twentieth century. No other trend has had such a colossal impact on every aspect of our lives . . . even conservatives now accept the general principle that race and sex should not preclude people from pursuing the profession they desire.[3]

Mister Rogers taught us thoughtful ways to respect and include different people when we were very young, and this reverence for the other
has grown into a mature moral system. Our greatest strength as young
people is our deference for diversity.

When it comes to religion, we understand that our path becomes
no less valid when we learn to see the validity of other paths. Respecting
the viewpoints of others does not diminish our own beliefs or crumble
our ethical foundation: "Love God with all of your heart, with all of
your mind and with all of your strength and love your neighbor as
you love yourself." In fact, the outcome of loving our neighbors as we
love ourselves seems to lead us to a deeper path of understanding and
appreciation of other faiths.

Two things propel this shift from an exclusive stance to a more
inclusive one: (1) we have humility concerning our thoughts about
God, and (2) we have seen how intolerance can result in violence.

Humility Concerning God

First, our respect for other faiths results from understanding the limits of our own knowledge. This is where a smattering of postmodern
thought is helpful in understanding younger generations, because the
philosophical change acknowledges that no one knows the fullness of
truth. Within the constant wordplay of this movement, there's a serious
confession that we cannot know anything entirely, especially God. We
spend our lives searching for understanding, but we see through a glass
darkly. Divine revelation is an unveiling process that assumes we will
never know the completeness of our immense God, so the exhilarating
and continual search for the divine is a lifetime process as we merely
scratch the surface in our understandings.

As young Christians approach religion, we know that Christianity
is true; yet, we also have the humble sense that our infinite God could
never be contained in our limited creeds or our most voluminous
theological libraries. We sense that God reveals Godself through other
cultures and other systems of thought.

The last few decades of theology have been extremely exciting,
as the dominant academic perspective has moved from talking about
God in a European context to inviting a multicultural perspective. Our

hermeneutics have been greatly enhanced by the challenges of women's voices. And our Christian views deepen as we enter into respectful dialogue with people of other faiths. Throughout these discussions, we realize that we may have one brilliant perspective on God, but divine character is much more varied than we can imagine, and so while we may have a glimpse of who God is, we know we cannot behold the face of God, and we can humbly admit that others may have a worthy perspective that broadens our own.

Intolerance and Violence

In addition to understanding our theological limits, we have a respect for other beliefs because we see the violence and destruction that occurs when religious groups focus on proselytizing and domination rather than building a just society. Throughout history, some of the world's most violent political acts can be blamed on religious intolerance. When we look at our political unrest through the lens of religion, the picture can be a devastating one. While driving through my neighborhood, I notice that my neighbors' bumper stickers have changed from "What Would Jesus Do?" to "Who Would Jesus Bomb?"

When terrible destruction occurred on U.S. soil, our nation had a gut urge to build up defenses, strike back, and repay someone for the immense acts of terrorism. But younger generations have been left to maintain security and rebuild the bombed-out Middle Eastern infrastructures. Whether it's portrayed on the television screen or crumpling right in front of them, many people in their twenties and thirties have seen too many civilian and military casualties and we yearn for another way.

A young soldier who recently returned from a peace-keeping mission to Iraq summed up the sentiment over breakfast a couple of months ago. He shook his head in disgust, "I drank beer with Iraqis. I know them. Our government does not understand their religion, and there's no keeping the peace over there until we can understand them."

People in their twenties and thirties use the Internet and text messaging to organize large demonstrations against the war. The common feelings and frustrations in these protests are that we have been lied to, that the lessons of combat have been devastating, and that we long to seek out common ground between peoples by understanding one another better.

So in this time of harsh violence, the church can begin meaningful dialogue with Jews and Muslims. Instead, intolerance too often begins in the church. We cannot feel truly human until we begin to have the strength to love and find some paths of forbearance and nonviolent resistance in our daily lives and, most important, in our spiritual communities.

In this important age, we can begin to see the value in other systems of thought, understand other faiths, and appreciate differing convictions. Younger generations can bring our churches and our broader society that much-needed gift of deference for diversity and respect for other religions. In a very real way, people in their twenties and thirties have learned who their neighbors are and can give us great insight in how to love them. Yet, if our churches keep up the fights, if we engage in fortifying our own systems of belief while invalidating and belittling the convictions of others, younger generations will not tolerate the intolerance and simply opt not to be a part of such churches.

Differing Sexual Orientations

Another way in which younger generations have learned to love their neighbors has been through an acceptance of differing sexual orientations. As a pastor, I have struggled with my congregations through many debates regarding homosexuality. I know where I stand, but I also realize the gut-wrenching wrestling that occurs in churches. Often the whole spectrum of belief sits in one sanctuary, and though I've spent sleepless nights worrying about the gay and lesbian members of our congregations, as a shepherd, I've never hoped that those who don't agree with me would go away. I couldn't simply dismiss those who believed that homosexuality was a sin. Thankfully, the wise and wonderful members of my congregation (including the gay and lesbian members) never expected me to.

The struggle that ministers endure through this debate can be devastating. I have seen wonderful pastors lose their parishes, and others nearly destroyed, because their views were much more inclusive than their churches'. I led one congregation that grappled with, prayed about, and tried to discern whether they should join the More Light movement of the Presbyterian Church (USA), an advocacy group striving for full inclusion of LGBT (lesbian, gay, bisexual and transgender) persons in our denomination. An elder entered my office, heartsick over the decision. He was progressive in his views on LGBT persons, but as a part of a small church, he was afraid that a couple of members would leave, and he grieved over that loss. He tried to work it out, saying, "But we are an open and affirming congregation—just look at our membership. Do we have to become part of a particular organization to prove it?"

With this question in mind, I had lunch with John Gage, a young and extraordinarily gifted UCC pastor who left the Presbyterian Church (USA) because of their exclusion of LGBT persons in positions of leadership, and now serves the United Church on the Green in Connecticut as his denomination's first openly gay senior minister. We ate soup at a busy New Haven coffee shop as I posed the question to him, "John, we're an open and affirming congregation, why do we need to become a part of a particular organization to prove it?"

"Because," he answered firmly, "gays and lesbians have been rejected by the church time and time again, and if we want to minister to our whole community, we need to confirm our stance as clearly as possible. We have to welcome them time and time again."

I sat back and understood. In this crucial point in church history, we are called to drown out the centuries of denials, dismissals, and refusals with unambiguous inclusion. The decision to fully include LGBT persons into our congregations not only affects the homosexuals in our society, but an entire generation.

Rebuffing the Majority

When a conservative Southern Baptist friend asked me about church growth, I told her that including LGBT persons was an important key to a healthy developing congregation.

"Carol, that can't be true," she responded. "Gays and lesbians only make up maybe two percent of the population. Including such a minority group can't make that big of a difference."

Of course, it's difficult to measure what percentage of the population is homosexual. In some regions, it might be as low as two or as high as six percent, and in other regions, much higher. But the statistics concerning the younger generation's attitudes toward LGBT persons are clear: 72 percent of people from eighteen to thirty think gay and lesbian relationships should be legal,[4] and 68 percent of seventeen to twenty nine year olds believe that gay couples should be allowed to marry or form civil unions.[5] High school students favor LGBT rights with much higher numbers and even more conviction, so we should expect a dramatically different voting landscape in the years to come.[6] Scholars suggest that the change in attitude among young people is because they are more likely to know someone who is (or know that someone is) gay or lesbian.

When the church fights over whether to accept gay and lesbian leadership, we do not fight over whether we are going to accept two to three percent of the population. We dismiss 72 percent of younger generations. This "issue" is simply not an issue for most people in their twenties and thirties; in fact, many no longer feel able to worship in a community that will not accept gays and lesbians, because that congregation cannot accept their relatives and dearest friends.

Younger clergy, frustrated with the timid steps that mainline denominations take, talk about biding their time, just waiting until the natural cycle of life occurs, in the hope that someday opinions will change. At this point, though, they feel drained.

Robin Long Sanderson, a thirty-three-year-old UCC pastor, has enormous interpersonal skills, and she relates across generations with ease. In ministry, she balances her acute sense of humor with boundless energy and love. Yet she sums up her feelings on the LGBT debates by admitting, "I'm tired of the conversation. Ten years ago, I was excited that the dialogue was going on, but it seems that now it's just the same dialogue over and over. As a young adult, I find it wearying. It's so obvious to me that this should be a nonissue at this point—much like ordaining women is now basically a nonissue in most mainline denominations."

The more we engage in this effort, the more worn out young leaders become with the seeming futility of the discussions. Many no longer engage in the conversations because they find them exasperating. Our churches have become culturally tainted as homophobic and inhospitable to people under forty.

In the Presbyterian Church (USA), there is a guideline in our Book of Order that states there must be chastity outside of marriage or a person cannot serve as a deacon, elder, or minister in our denomination. This amendment affects gay and lesbians as well as anyone who has sex outside of marriage. Young adults put off marriage (but not sex) until they are in their mid-thirties, which means this amendment easily bans a majority of twenty- and thirty-year-olds from being deacons, elders, and pastors.

This change to our constitution passed when I was in seminary and I thought long and hard about what I should do. I decided to stay in our denomination, hoping that the rule would only be on the books for a short time before it would be overturned. It's been a decade now. There has been great debate and a tremendous struggle, but the amendment stands.

I have been in governing bodies where we debate the ordination of gay and lesbian Christians, and I often hear how the Bible should be the final authority on the issue. Yet, our holy Scriptures are culturally bound, and many of its attitudes toward women, slaves, and people of non-Jewish ethnicities appall modern sensibilities. Customs concerning disease, menstruation, and childbirth are outrageous to our twenty-first century understanding. Both conservative and liberal readers of the Bible learn to disregard certain customs and traditions in the text because they were specific to that particular time and place.

This is certainly the case with human sexuality; in fact, sexual norms may be the most fluid aspect of scriptural instruction. The ideas of human sexuality alter drastically from Abraham's relationship with Hagar, his wife's slave; to David's marriages for political alliance; to Solomon's insatiable sexual appetite for seven hundred concubines; to Esther's brave rise from the harem to the throne; to Ruth's seduction of her kinsman redeemer; to Paul's insistence that church leaders remain single (unless they "burn").

Even with the evolving notions in the text, our mainline denominations uphold this divisive stance on sexuality time and time again, not realizing the devastating effect our intolerance has on the young adults in our congregations.

In the years to come, if churches are going to minister to people in their twenties and thirties, we will look for ways to make a space for them, their friends, and their relatives. It is not necessary that everyone in our denominations agree with them, but it is necessary that congregations make room for differing opinions. Churches can no longer stand at the velvet ropes, banning young adults from worship. I hope we will have the courage to override the centuries of dismissals, denials, and refusals, and welcome each person as a good neighbor.

Spiritual, Not Religious

A few weeks ago, a couple entered my mossy green office, wanting to get married. As they sat down on the couch, I noticed that they represented the diverse and wonderful trends that I find in many modern couples: they were in their late thirties and from two different parts of the globe. As we spoke, they explained that they lived far from their families of origin and had met over the Internet. The bride grew up Presbyterian, so it meant a lot for her to be married by a Presbyterian clergyperson. When I asked about the groom's background, he moved to the edge of the couch, "Well, there's something you need to understand," he began. "I'm not really a religious person. I'm more of a spiritual person."

I understood. For one thing, many people who find out about my profession make this quick confession. When I first began hearing it, I was in seminary, so thickly embedded in my love for theology and church history that I always had the urge to respond with good old-fashioned eye-rolling. I immediately assumed that the person's central spiritual practice was watching Oprah on a Thursday afternoon. But, I kept hearing it more and more from people my age who were inside and outside of the church: "I'm not really a religious person. I'm more of a spiritual person." Finally, I began to listen.

Our generation has a vague view of religion that we discern from the public forum: evangelists on the television defending prayer in school, wanting the ten commandments on the walls of our courthouses, and promoting intelligent design; picketers in front of abortion clinics yelling out "murderer" to a scared teenage girl; and fanatics outside the funerals of homosexual college students holding signs that read "GOD HATES GAYS." There is a Christian-led struggle against stem cell research and birth control. Religious family groups demonize mothers who have meaningful careers. We see a street preacher, setting up his sound systems on 42nd Street in New York City. With a heavy Bible in one hand and a screechy microphone in another, he yells at the crowd, condemning them to hell. There are Muslim suicide bombers, Jewish military forces, and pedophile priests. If someone in their twenties and thirties has a positive view of religion after living through the events of the last couple of decades, they've overcome some huge obstacles.

Moderate and progressive Christians seem to be absent from societal struggles. Maybe we're not as good at getting news coverage, or we're spending too much time with our ingrown denominational battles, or we're worrying too much about our own decline that we don't have any effect on our society. When the mainline does make the news, it's arguing over sex or property.

As a result, "being religious" has become synonymous with being small-minded, belligerent, arrogant, perverse, and even violent. As one friend admitted to me, "I don't go to church because it just seemed like a place where they told me, 'Don't run. Don't be gay. Get a haircut.'" When he got older, he really didn't see the sense in it. This church's stance contradicts those important values of tolerance, compromise, and humility. So, with great collective wisdom, younger generations found another way. They began identifying more with the movement of the Spirit, rather than the rules of the institution. When a young person explains that she is more spiritual than religious, she wants to take a step back from the intolerance and hypocrisy of modern institutions and emphasize orthopraxis over orthodoxy; in other words, younger generations are much more interested in right practice than right belief.[7]

While the frustrations with our institutions have caused younger generations to distance themselves from religion, they do embrace spirituality. They are more attracted to the discipline of communicating with God than getting the list of attributes of God completely correct. Less concerned with obtaining the true literal interpretation of the Bible, they are more engrossed by what the text means to them and how they can live out an authentic faith. Not anxious about controlling the thoughts of others, they have a faith that seeks to understand our nurturing God. They question the notion that our particular brand of

Christianity is the only worthy path, so they embrace the wider term "spirituality" which recognizes that God works through a variety of cultures and beliefs. With a growing sense that God has a purpose for us, they long to discern their way according to God's direction. They reject the pressures in our society that foster waste and abuse of the earth and look for ways to observe more responsible, simple lifestyles. They will not stand with those who write up an exclusionary list of who can enter the doors of the church; instead, they have found vast beauty in a diversity of thought, and great meaning in practicing what Jesus taught. It all comes down to this: "Love God with all of your heart, all of your soul and all of your mind," "love your neighbor as you love yourself," and "do to others as you would have them do to you."

Right Practice

I am reminded of this shift from orthodoxy to orthopraxis when I practice walking meditation. "It is solved by walking," Augustine wrote, and I take the instruction seriously as I slip on my shoes and find my way to the nearest green space in the city. After years of trying to set aside some silent time to sit in a bare room to pray, I learned that I'm like one of those nervous coaches at the edge of the basketball court, I think best on my feet and I pray on my feet too. I still have a regular practice of Scripture reading and contemplative prayer, but I feel much more connected to God as I pace my steps on the twisted path that runs through the trees.

When I make eye contact with a deer leading her babies through that strip of forest, I know that I am a fragment of something larger than myself and I begin to sense my part in God's good creation. Nature always surprises me, and I am enthralled as I share a bit of the trail with the silky blue gecko.

Abruptly, I trip and catch myself before I hit the ground. Looking down, I notice that knobs of roots emerge from the dust. Their strange pattern looks like a mushroom village and I stop to wonder why they grew up instead of down, making knees like the ones in the swamps of Louisiana. I crouch and realize that water used to flow over that area until it organized into a small stream. To my right, the constant trickling current courses through a deep gorge. The power of the water cuts through the ground, leaving layers of earth exposed like thick lasagna served in a glass casserole dish. I sit down, fascinated by the complicated root system, which moves around the rock and soil, and the force of the small stream that slices right through it all.

I begin to think about the church. Everything constantly changes around us. Even the most basic things in our lives like the way we communicate with friends or where we live are quickly shifting. We never step into the same river twice. Yet, somehow in this vital generation, this fluid motion exposes the roots that ground us. When all of the extraneous soil has been cut back, we long to be spiritual people, anchored in our life-giving traditions. We are left with the heart of our practice: to love God and love our neighbor.

As churches form spiritual communities for the missing generations, we begin to see the roots of right practice. For many, it feels like an upheaval of moral and cultural norms, a philosophical shift from any sort of foundation; but for other people in their twenties and thirties, this powerful movement cuts back religion's intolerance and their own bitter cynicism to reveal the rich history of our spiritual traditions that connect us with God and one another.

We are a generation that is more spiritual than religious, and as our mainline churches begin to hear this and receive the gifts that younger generations bring, we will experience a movement that anchors us and binds us together in extraordinary ways of unambiguous inclusion.

Reflection Questions

1. What do you think about the statement, "I'm more of a spiritual person than a religious person"?
2. What do you think about a shift of emphasis from orthodoxy (right belief) to orthopraxis (right practice)? Is there a way that we can have a strong focus on orthodoxy and tolerance?
3. What sort of influences shaped your attitudes toward sexuality and other faith traditions? Have you changed your views? Tell a story about how your opinions became different.

4. What makes you worried about the views of younger generations? What makes you hopeful about the views of younger generations?

CHAPTER 5

Discovering
Affirming
Traditions

Charlotte's mother taught her how to swim by throwing her into the pool because she'd heard that was the best way to train an infant not to drown. The baby learned to keep her head above the surface; in fact, Charlotte even became a strong swimmer. But, as is the case with many childhood traumas, she also acquired a great deal of fear that eventually marked the paths of her emotions.

Panic overtook her in logical situations, like when she watched her son swim in the shallow waters of a hotel pool. She would feel the hot sun stinging her back and then a cold shaky feeling gripping her neck, until she reminded herself that the fear stemmed from her own experiences, that it had nothing to do with her child's safety, and that she could begin breathing normally again.

The anxiety struck at illogical times, like when Charlotte moved to a new town. She remained at the perimeter of the neighborhood, reluctant to become engaged in the community, with her gut churning, wondering if she would be overwhelmed by her loneliness and alienation. One afternoon, the fright intensified when Charlotte was filling out her son's school registration papers and couldn't think of a single person she could list as an emergency contact.

When she drifted to sleep that evening, Charlotte dreamed that she was dropped into the pool again and no longer knew how to swim with flowing strokes; instead, she reverted back to the short, choppy moves that had barely kept her from drowning. She reached out, gasping and hoping that someone would be there at the end of her fingertips, but no one rescued her. Upon waking, the longing lingered. She yearned for some sort of support—an emotional, physical and spiritual bond—as she entered the fluid surroundings of her new neighborhood. Charlotte wanted connection with God, a community, and her neighbors.

Connection with God

Charlotte was seeking to be more deeply anchored in the grounding relationship with the Creator, Christ, and the Holy Spirit. For many disconnected people, affirming traditions secure us. When we reach back into the rich history of our church, we can learn those rhythms that offer meaning to our Ordinary Days. When we begin to walk and pray, our connection with God grows and we become aware of our vital part in God's good creation. We understand the importance of caring for the earth and how the richness of the rocks and soil below us reflects the abundant imagination of our Creator.

As we engage in spiritual practices, welcoming the stranger at our door, seeking discernment in our decisions and meditating on the germane wisdom of Jesus's teachings, we begin to understand how to love God with each step we take. As we recognize our part in the body of Christ and understand our callings within it, we start to realize who our neighbor is and what it means to love her.

Learning to become comfortable in silence, we can sense the Holy Spirit working in and among us, strengthening the bonds of community in our most diverse settings. The Spirit emboldens us to seek justice and mercy in our society.

Our spiritual communities hold these practices in our bellies, and as we dig deeply to engage in these important traditions, the ground beneath us becomes firm. We will not always know where we need to place our next step, but we will become more certain of the solid soil of the present moment.

God forms our communities in the faithful repetition of prayer, Scripture reading, meditation, and worship which is typically centered around baptism and the Eucharist or Communion. The seasons or calendar of the church give us an internal compass that guides us into times of growth, contemplation, fasting, lament, remorse, and celebration.

Walking alongside the Worshiper

Of course, our most important tradition is Sunday morning worship. This is the main entry point that we have with new people and we do well to realize that many people are experiencing and learning the church's traditions from scratch. Yet, the order of worship can be confounding to even the most practiced individuals; even with a Master of Divinity degree, at times I find it confusing to walk into a new church and follow the liturgy. Sometimes I've wondered if worship services are subtly intended to weed out people with the wrong sort of background.

My suspicion became a little clearer when I sat in a church growth seminar that my husband, Brian Merritt, was teaching. He suggested that the lectionary reader could announce the page number of the scripture passage to make people feel comfortable in the service, and one participant responded, "That's where I draw the line. If a person can't look things up in the Bible, then he shouldn't be in church!"

When a person begins to worship in a different setting, she not only has to know where all the books in the Bible are, she has to know when to sit, stand, and kneel; how to read music; how to take communion; how to pray the Lord's Prayer, recite the Apostles' Creed, and respond to the Great Prayer of Thanksgiving; how to sing the "Doxology"; and how to look things up in the prayer book. With 18 percent of college freshmen never having attended a church service in their lives, is it any wonder young people feel so completely disoriented in mainline denominational church services?[1]

When I pastored a congregation in Abbeville, Louisiana, I became very aware of how exclusive our liturgy could be. After studying how high the illiteracy rate was in our small town, I cut out the complicated readings and began to incorporate simple repetitive responses to prayer. I learned quickly that if I wanted to effectively minister to the community, I couldn't start out by embarrassing 40 percent of the potential congregation during the opening prayer.

We can look for ways to carry the worshiper with us through the service. If a prayer will be offered in unison, it can be printed in the order of service. If a creed will be affirmed by the whole congregation, we can write down the words or note the page. If the congregation expects the worshiper to read along with the text, the Scripture can be included in the bulletin or the place in which it's found can be announced.

Churches can look for opportunities to listen to new visitors (or a rarely seen, disgruntled spouse of a member) and note the things that they find confusing within the first year. This is a vital time for the new person, because after twelve months she will get into the rhythm of things and forget what she did not know when she walked into the sanctuary. But during those initial months, her irritation can be very instructive for the worshiping community. The new person can point out all the confusing elements in our orders of worship and help the liturgy to become what it is intended to be: the work of the people.

Connection with a Spiritual Community

Sunday morning worship is our central affirming tradition. Yet, other things will also grow up alongside the service, and these can be wonderful new traditions. At Western Presbyterian Church, we have a tradition of taking students out to Easter brunch. The first year I was in charge of the meal, I planned for a small handful of people and wondered if that many would even show up. I made arrangements with a restaurant the students picked, located about a mile away from the church. By the time we walked to Mimi's Bistro, our crowd of students had rapidly grown and I called from my cell phone to multiply our reservation by four.

After we sat down, people kept trickling in, so we kept scooting closer to each other in the booths and squeezing in more silverware. Looking around the Bistro I noticed neon papier-mâché dragons hanging from the black ceiling and giant sketchy murals adorning the walls. The animated staff looked like actors of some sort, waiting on their tables as well as for their big break. We each ordered some variation of eggs benedict and waited for hours for the food to arrive.

The restaurant grew louder and I saw that our lunch invitation had brought not only students but a number of other young adults, recent graduates who had attended this brunch with the church for years. It was their Easter custom, and so it continued. Young men and women surrounded me, talking and laughing. Every once in a while, they were reminded of the looming project, fifteen-page paper, or final thesis that they needed to complete, but for the most part, they just celebrated Easter and repeatedly thanked me for the opportunity to be together when they could not be with their families.

By the time we walked back to the church, our numbers had dwindled back to the original size. Noticing all of the stranded lilies and tulips in the sanctuary, I gave them to students to take home. As I wished them a happy Easter one more time, I realized that in this custom, the resurrection of Jesus had become much more meaningful—even incarnational—as the friends gathered for a meal together. Our connection as a spiritual community deepened as the church allowed students to have space and a custom in which a tribe could develop.

THE INVISIBLE RULEBOOK

As a spiritual community begins to weave younger people into its life, as tribes begin to form in our midst, we will need traditions. Though there will be traditions common to the larger congregational tribe, others will be peculiar to each particular tribe. All tribes have rites of passage, seasonal celebrations and practices that enhance their bond, and young generations also need affirming traditions where we can form a deeper connection with God, each other, and the world. At the same time, the traditions need to value our contributions and consider our schedules as working people and parents.

There is an important difference between the customs and the traditions in our church, which Diana Butler Bass points out in her book *The Practicing Congregation,*

> Custom refers to what people do, actions in accordance with precedent; tradition refers to that which accompanies the action. Customs may (and often must) change, whereas traditions are forms of belief and practice that are understood to have longer historical

grounding linked to some more ancient and universal source of
authority and meaning.[2]

We have many customs in our churches: the yard sales, ham dinners,
and craft shows, the annual fundraisers and regular social occasions.
Often, when young members begin to attend a small congregation, a
great sigh of relief echoes through the sanctuary because the membership anticipates a sharing of the burden. The enormous amount of
work that it takes to pull these annual events together will be spread
out among more people—and specifically young people, with lots of
energy and ambition.

So, the chair of the yard sale committee begins to recruit this new
blood as soon as they begin to get settled in their spiritual home. The
church wants to assimilate that fresh face, give him an assignment, and
make him feel like he is a useful part of things. Sometimes this works
beautifully. The additional person becomes involved and active, rolling
up his sleeves and serving in the line at the spaghetti dinner. But most
of the time it doesn't work.

Who's to blame? Is it the new member, who finishes his assigned
task, but promises himself, "never again"? Is it the older member, who
just wants to get that young man involved in the life of the church?
The fault does not rest easily on either well-intentioned party; instead,
there is something else in the equation, something that has become
such an essential part of the custom that we do not even recognize that
it exists. It's the invisible rulebook.

We attach these rulebooks to every event, and they regulate the
price of tickets, where tables should be set up and by whom, and how
funds should be collected and allocated. The guidelines take years to
gather and they are written in the murky history of the yard sale committee, in the collective unconscious of the planning team. When a new
person (let's call him Tom) comes in, he is not yet familiar with this
unwritten congregational book and will unwittingly break all kinds of
sacred rules. Tom will suggest that the tables be set by the window, instead of the door. He will want the money to go to the homeless shelter,
instead of the children's home. Tom will make many of the mistakes
that the church has made and corrected over the last fifty years.

After a couple of meetings where several of his ideas are met with, "No, we tried that before," or "We couldn't possibly do that," or "That just doesn't work," Tom is quickly conditioned. He learns that he will not make a significant contribution to the project and his valuable time would be better spent doing something else. Tom's a lot smarter than Pavlov's dogs and he knows that repeated negative responses means that he would be better off leaving the task for others.

Time is costly for all of us, but it seems especially precious for younger generations. Whereas a family in the past could be supported by one forty-hour job, now it often takes more than eighty hours of labor. The moments that we have left for our children and our own spiritual enrichment get smaller and smaller each year. Plus the cost of childcare is substantial (the average rate is $12 to $16 per hour in my neighborhood), which means that those two-hour planning meetings, where all of his ideas were rejected, may have cost Tom valuable time as well as $56.[3] And that was just to get started.

Yet when we do fundraisers as a church, the first rule in that invisible book is that that church members must disregard the amount of time it takes to make the money because the project is more for the companionship than how much money is produced. So when the church spends 3,000 accumulated hours to produce $350 for a mission project, it might be considered a great success for retired members with no babysitting to pay for, but the project leaves younger members aggravated by the disturbing labor-to-production ratio.

That is not to say that younger members view everything through a "time is money" frame. We often need a break from our productive lives. Our souls require rest and an occasion to heal from the fracturing stress of our days. We yearn for a place where silence and simplicity are taught and valued, where our connection with God and each other can strengthen. We long for a space where our deepest spiritual longings can be attended to through enriching practices—with childcare provided.

For established members of the congregation, customs are important because relationships blossomed around those tasks and often the church's identity in the community is wrapped up in a certain event.

"I'm pretty sure that my church exists for their chicken salad sup-per," one pastor in the West confided to me, only half joking. "When I began as a pastor, they had this table sitting in the corner of the fel-lowship hall. When I asked, 'What's this table doing here?' someone in my congregation quickly answered, 'You can't move that! It's for the Chicken Salad Supper!' Oh, and did I mention? The table had no legs!"

As new generations gather in a church, vital congregations learn to adapt their customs while keeping their traditions. While the energy might dwindle around the yard sale, it's important to keep the practice of generosity and kindness intact. Realizing that their present social and economic structure may not always be able to support rummage retailing, they need to find ways to nurture their love for their neighbor. Acknowledging the need to care for creation and be wise about how they dispose of things, they can look for other ways to clean out closets and recycle their unwanted items.

Connection with the World

Tribes thrive when renewing their connection with God through artist groups, contemplation groups, and spirituality groups. They flourish when they maintain connection with each other, realizing their part in the body of Christ through picnics, lunches, and hikes. And tribes form as they connect with the world and respond to social justice issues.

For younger generations, "mission" is more of a verb rather than a noun. Rather than referring simply to writing a check, it means getting out and doing something like feeding the homeless in soup kitchens, caring for the sick through AIDS teams, cultivating a community gar-den, or working with Habitat for Humanity.

Miriam's Kitchen, a feeding and social services program housed at Western Presbyterian Church, where I pastor in D.C., has learned to build connections with their homeless clients and with their young volunteers. The executive director, Scott Schenkelberg, told me, "Bob Putnam's right. Our generation is 'bowling alone.' We see it. When people volunteer at the kitchen, they're not just looking for a place to feed the homeless; they're looking for a place to build a community."[4]

Recognizing this important ingredient, the staff of Miriam's holds regular volunteer appreciation events, like tailgate parties at baseball games and barbecues in the church courtyard. Largely attended by people in their twenties and thirties, the gatherings become a place where people can meet like-minded and caring people at least as much as be honored for their volunteer contributions.

Forming Affirming Traditions

Church members want new people to attend the church because they hope to lighten the load in fundraising events, keep dwindling programs alive, and support the diminishing budget. Sometimes it happens that way, but more often, if the members become intentional about ministering to younger generations, they will move away from assimilating the new people into existing customs and begin a process of forming new communities. The body will become aware of the gifts and needs of that particular group and respond to them by teaching the traditions of belief and practice in a more fluid, not rigid, way. The congregation will rest from the drive to brand the members with denominational labels and become open to forming affirming traditions.

The process of formation occurs in a strange manner. It's a regular practice that requires discipline and study; a link to that ancient, solid ground. Then, within this stable structure, something grows, but we can't predict how and when we'll sense God's presence. Diana Butler Bass calls this process "fluid retraditioning."[5] In *The Practicing Congregation*, Bass details how a spiritual movement has given mainline churches vitality in the past decade. I have seen that new life in groups of younger members.

In the midst of this spiritual renewal, it's difficult to point out the steps of the process. Instead, forming spiritual communities is like painting: an artist sketches regularly, studies objects and figures, learns from the great works of history, and shows up at the sketchbook or canvas each day. Much of what she produces may be inconsequential, but then suddenly something begins to move within her. She picks up the brush, after some time she feels stirred internally and externally, and creates a work of great beauty. That jolt of inspiration seemed to come out of a clear blue sky. And it did, in some ways. But it also came out of the careful discipline that opens a person to immanent revelation. In the same way, if churches lead people into practicing disciplines, something will begin to grow up.

I saw this happen in Barrington, Rhode Island, too, when a couple of families decided to go camping. We announced it for weeks in the service, but no one seemed interested in the adventure. The night before the trip, we decided to cancel, due to a lack of involvement. So I was surprised the next year when the camping idea came up again.

By that time, more families had joined the church, and two of them were true outdoors people. They had every bit of camping equipment that one could ever desire or require. They set up their tents so often that they knew every site in the state, and they wisely chose a spot called "The Whispering Pines" that provided hot showers, a swimming pool, children's activities, and a pancake breakfast.

We trudged out to the wilderness, set up our tents, and blew up our air mattresses. Many children of the church had never been camping before, and they brimmed with excitement. Unfortunately, the thrill never wore off that night. One toddler could not get to sleep, knowing that her church friends were so close by, so she jumped on her parent's air mattress until 11:00 at night. At three a.m., she realized with glee that she was still there, in that tent, so she began her gymnastics routine again. Her mom had to drag her into the minivan where she read to her for the rest of the weary morning.

Another family could not get their boys to sleep in the tent, so they buckled the kids up in their car seats and drove them around and around the empty highways for hours until the children finally gave in to sleep. Each zombie-like parent had a horror story that they unfolded over the pancakes, pool activities, and sidewalk drawings.

At the end of the day, I was about to chalk the trip up to another creative disaster (and there have been many creative disasters), until I walked back to my tent and began to smell Italian food cooking and a campfire smoking. Our friends had this giant meal of spaghetti heating up on their Coleman kitchen set, and their coolers were still full of every imaginable drink. We all gathered to fill our plates with pasta and meatballs. With all the fresh air of that day, spaghetti never looked so good.

Before we began to eat, Calla, my then-four-year-old daughter, led us in a prayer that she had learned from Madeline, one of her favorite children's book characters:

We love our bread, we love our butter,
But most of all we love each other.
Amen.

For a split second, there was complete silence—until a pair of sisters sang a beautiful blessing to the tune of Frère Jacques and invited us to join in the round. Next, a twelve-year-old boy, who had recently attended a retreat on prayer, called out a quick verse and smiled broadly. As the sun set and the crickets began their whistling, the kids taught their prayers, the adults reached back for the simple poems of gratitude and faith that formed them as children, and we shared the ones that we were learning.

With those words of thanksgiving flowing up among us, we witnessed how inviting God to our tables could change an ordinary meal to a sacred one. I sat at the gray wooden picnic table, swatting mosquitoes, munching on garlic bread, and nodding happily. It had happened in that moment, in the midst of our sacred traditions that sprang up from the children and their parents; we sensed the Holy Spirit blowing through those whispering pines. I knew that, despite the restless night, the church would have the camping trip again, because an important tradition formed when we sensed our connection with God, each other, and the world. The outing became more than a custom, because God formed a new community through our ancient tradition of prayer.

These moments—when we feel as if we are a part of something larger than ourselves and we sense our connection to God and our neighbor—these moments feed us. In our hunger, when we cannot grasp on to anything else at the end of our fingertips, we long for these rare Spirit-filled times. They are the reason that younger generations go to church.

For a generation filled with submerging people like Charlotte, affirming traditions of prayer, meditation, and worship give us grounding in our fluid surroundings. For students and young families, the firm earth gives us the constant rhythm, seasons of celebration that order our chaotic lives. In our worship and our life together, these ancient anchors connect us with our divine source of vitality, and with that foundation we can extend God's care to the world. With the affirming traditions of a spiritual community, we feel something at our fingertips. When we reach up and out, we continue to learn what it means to love God and love our neighbor.

Reflection Questions

1. What spiritual practices have helped you in the past? What ordinary things do you do that help you maintain a sense of wholeness (for example, washing the dishes, walking to work, regularly drinking a cup of tea with a friend)?
2. Do you have church events that have an invisible rulebook attached to them? What important role does it play in the life of the congregation? What are the core spiritual values that the function produces? If the energy is drained around the event, what other ways can your congregation continue to practice those core traditions?
3. In your congregation, when have you sensed a connection with God? What communal practices would you like to see happen or increase in the future?
4. Within the life of your church, what traditions do you have that encourage new people to make friends? What sort of gatherings would you like to see in the next five years that would encourage those bonds?
5. How does your congregation connect with the world? What are your mission practices? Are there opportunities beyond giving money? What are the ministries around which your congregation has the most energy and passion?

CHAPTER 6

Promoting Shared Leadership

I taught the last confirmation class at my house. The thirteen-year-olds munched on Papa John's pizza as we discussed the Trinity, how to pray, and church polity. I didn't go into a full description of the constitution of the church, just the basic things that they needed to know, like the importance of lay people in our church government. I explained that "Presbyterian" comes from the Greek word πρεσβυτεριον, which means "elder."

"Oh!" exclaimed Shelley, who'd stopped chewing her pepperoni and wore one of those faces that every teacher longs for, that one which indicated that she finally got it. "So that's why everyone running our church is so old!"

My smile fell. Teenagers have an amazing knack for truth-telling.

The Denominational Lifespan

Shelley grew up in a congregation, so she was living out the lifespan and rituals of a mainline denominational person: after she was born, the church baptized her and cared for her. When she came of age, she entered confirmation class (which she enjoyed, by the way). Then, we can expect, she would not attend church again—for years. The church would miss her adult face forming and she would grow another four inches, so we will hardly recognize her when she shows up for the candlelight Christmas Eve service. When she leaves for college, the church will receive occasional dispatches from her parents and be told when she graduates. Then, the congregation will hope that she comes back after her first child is born, maybe when she is in her thirties—after spending a couple of decades away from a spiritual community. Perhaps she will meet a nice mainline guy, or maybe that confirmation class will stick, or maybe there will be some denominational loyalty and Shelley will remember to wander back into our doors so that we can reap the benefit of her Presbyterian upbringing.

She will spend her late thirties kind of getting the hang of attending again, although it will be pretty hard because of the kids—their vacation schedule and soccer practice will always be in the way of becoming regular attendees. Learning her confirmation lessons well, Shelley will realize again that the church is like the Masons, Shriners and Garden Club: it is run by older people.

Then, when her children are grown, and Shelley has more time on her hands, she will start getting involved. In her late fifties, she will begin leading the church in meaningful ways. After she retires, she will look into heading up a committee within higher governing bodies, and she will continue to guide the denomination until the end of her life.[1]

For most people, this is not an ideal way to form one's spiritual life. Teenagers have great needs as they make important decisions that will affect the rest of their lives; they begin habits and make lifestyle choices that they will have to nurture or break in the years to come. College students often require a spiritual community as they leave home and discern their educational paths. Career starters rely on the church as they begin to prioritize their values and navigate through confusing romantic relationships. In the most crucial times in a person's life, the mainline denominational church has acquiesced to the life-cycle: they have conceded to take care of the babies and the elderly, but give up on anything in between. The church lets go of young people when they need spiritual grounding the most.

I've had conversations with many mainline leaders who feel completely comfortable with a denominational lifespan that includes a twenty-year hibernation period from the church. Having resigned themselves to it a long time ago, they figure that this is just the way it works. They assume that people will return in good time and rely on denominational branding to lead them back. They are comfortable with retired people running every aspect of church life.

Yet, the waning prospects of our mainline denominations shows that the life-cycle is not good for our churches.[2] An estimated two-thirds of all Baby Boomers who were brought up in the church dropped out, and less than half of them returned.[3] And what about their children? We need the gifts and vision of younger people: the prophetic insight and deep fervor of teenagers, the determination and drive of college students and career starters, and the planning and attention of young families. Our churches become anemic without these vital generations serving and leading us.

While most congregations fret over the trend of religious drop-outs and aging religious leaders, they feel like there is nothing they can do about it. They simply do not understand why there's a lack of young leaders in their midst. In the following pages, we will look at a couple of reasons for the deficiency of young leaders in our local churches, examine the struggles that intergenerational leadership can cause, and look at some hopeful solutions. Then we will look at the particular problems that young clergy face and offer some guidance.

Excused Absence

As a pastor in a mainline denominational church, I see two things that encourage our people to drop out and that stand in the way of building up young leadership: (1) people hold on to positions of leadership, and (2) the church disregards the presence and resources of twenty- and thirty-year-olds when they do show up.

Letting Go of Leadership Positions

From our congregational pews to our pulpits to our denominational gatherings, older generations have obtained and held fast to their power. When they pass retirement age, their grip seems to tighten around their positions. As people live longer, they cling to them even more. The effect has been a general aging of our leadership. When I attended a denominational meeting with a twenty-seven-year old lay leader, she left saying, "that was a very scary experience for someone like me" because of the overwhelming presence of septuagenarians. While churches lament over a leadership crisis, older members spend so much of their energy on running institutions that it makes them blind to the potential leaders in their midst.

People live longer, with great strength and vitality. In 2003, the glowing Lauren Hutton graced the cover of AARP with the headline "Sixty is the New Thirty." While grandmothers used to do a little light dusting in their twilight years, now grandmothers are far away from the dust and the dusk as they take up biking, hiking, and mountain climbing—or continue in the workplace. When an elder exceeds her retirement age in the workplace, she has tremendous energy, and it has been a wonderful gift for the church to have retired people in leadership positions. They have taken up the duties that young women can no longer do since they have entered the workforce. Most people who hold on to positions of power do it because they do not see anyone who could take their place, and surely our churches could not function without the wisdom and life of older generations.

But if sixty is the new thirty, have we left any room in our churches for the actual thirty-year-olds? Certainly we have not allowed much denominational power to rest in their able hands. If we want to have younger generations in our pews, then we can begin by receiving them in our pulpits and on our boards and committees, by asking them to take up leadership positions, and by sharing power with them.

Valuing the Resources of the Young

We often disregard the important assets that adults under forty can offer us. In the denominational church, leadership positions are given to people who prove themselves in some way. Usually they're people who have a great deal of influence, time, or money. This makes sense. As a church builds its leadership, as pastors and committees search congregations for elders and deacons, they look for the strongest possible links to make up that leadership chain, and if that person has established themselves in a community by gaining power, donating time, or giving money, then it's likely that they will be a solid leader in the church. They will use their influence positively, put in the valuable hours, and devote their resources to the work and mission of the church. Every congregation needs these important commodities to minister effectively.

The problem is that young people usually do not have power, time, or money. But they have other things: potential, creativity, imagination, vision, and ideas. As the modern philosopher Hannah Arendt explains in *The Life of the Mind*, if we look at a person's lifespan in a linear fashion, we can see that a person at the beginning of the line looks forward, while a person at the end of the line looks backward.[4] Younger people have a natural orientation toward planning while older people have an inclination to reminisce.

If we follow Hannah Arendt's logic as a general rule—a rule that has many, many exceptions—we might understand that young people are planners, while older people are historians. Since our denominational churches have so many older people in leadership, we become trapped in a pattern where we desire the past: conservatives pine away for the 1950s and liberals long for the 1960s.

This becomes clear in the photographs we display in our fellowship hall. We place the black and white photos on our walls, and look at how our congregations used to be, with hundreds of people lined up in front of the doors of the church, with all of the young families and children, hands to their sides, hair neatly combed, and leather shoes shining. It's wonderful to learn about these important periods in our history. But if the energy, vision, and wall space of the church focuses on recreating a time when the congregation's present young people were not even alive, trying to be part of a church becomes understandably frustrating for those in their twenties and thirties.

I remember being in seminary, constantly hearing about the days of mainline denominational glory, when prominent Protestant theologians made it on to the cover of Time magazine. I heard so many stories about the civil rights movement that I felt like I was sinking in the midst of this institutional longing for the past. A popular song by Jesus Jones was getting a lot of air time on the radio, and although Jesus Jones isn't one of my favorite artists, each time this particular song played, I turned up my stereo as loud as I could bear it and would belt out the chorus:

Right here, right now, there is no other place I'd rather be.
Right here, right now, watching the world wake up from history.

You see, I wanted to enjoy my youth while I was still living it. I didn't want to spend my time yearning for someone else's glory days, and I was certainly not interested in going through an institutional midlife crisis in my twenties.

A leadership crisis exists, but it's not because of a lack of talent and resources from younger generations, it's because the church can get so caught up in trying to recreate those Norman Rockwell days that we forget to look at where we are right here, right now. While the Baby Boomers used to say, "Never trust anyone over thirty," now their motto seems to be "never trust anyone under thirty."

Breaking the Life-Cycle

Joyce Smedburg, a wonderful community leader who affected hundreds of young lives in Riverside, Rhode Island, let me in on the secret to her successful calling: "You just treat young people like they're people. That's all." So, the way that we can keep Shelley, our confirmation student, engaged in her twenties is the same way that we can keep Shelley engaged in her sixties: let her run the church. Once a young woman turns sixteen, she can hardly bear to sit in the back seat of the car. She wants to drive. Just like any person, she wants to feel like she can contribute to the leadership of the church and wants to have some say in the decisions of the congregation. And the church needs her opinions; the congregation needs her to take the steering wheel when she's thirteen, eighteen, twenty-six, and eighty-five.

This looks different in different congregations. At Westminster Presbyterian Church in Austin, Texas, when Laura Mendenhal was the pastor, children could always be found serving as greeters and ushers, and there was often a teenager or college student reading the Scripture passages.

In Barrington Presbyterian Church in Rhode Island, the youth met before the service to plan the children's sermon and special services, like the Maundy Thursday and Christmas Eve services. They came up with wonderful ways to minister to our congregation through writing prayers, providing special music, and leading the liturgy. Our creative group of teenagers even figured out how to turn water into wine. During one children's sermon, they poured water from a crystal decanter into a clear wine glass that had the perfect number of red and blue food coloring drops in the bottom of it. Miraculously, the wine appeared in the glass as we told the story of Jesus's first miracle.

It's important that we have visible signs that every age group is involved in our churches, but we have to do more than allow the surface to look young. We must entrust people under forty with some power and let them claim their authority.

King of the Mountain

Richard, an elder at a Presbyterian Church in a rural farming town in Kentucky, learned this lesson well. He began his term in turmoil. Before a congregational meeting, someone asked him if he would like to be an elder. "Of course, I'd be happy to serve," was Richard's quick reply.

So, after the nominating committee gave their report, listing the names of the usual suspects, mostly elders from one particular family in the congregation, the moderator opened the floor to any other nominations, and a man sitting in the front row raised his hand and stood up, "Yes. I have a nomination. I would like to propose Richard."

A rumble began in the congregation. Although this was a perfectly sound parliamentary move, it was unprecedented in this country church, which had always voted unanimously on the unaltered ballot presented by the nominating committee. Consequently, there was little change among the elders. The session members rotated off for a year after their second term, of course, but they unfailingly returned to serve. The surprise nomination hoped to break this pattern.

Richard was a relatively new person in the congregation, a physician who had begun attending with his family two years earlier. He was one of the first of a steady stream of young adults who joined the church as the little village became a bedroom community for the nearby city. Although Richard had grown up in the area, he was still part of a dynamic demographic shift of younger, highly educated families looking for affordable housing farther from their workplace. The congregation hoped to attract those young families to their church, but they did not realize the implications of actually having them there.

After the moderator called the congregation to order, they took the vote, and Richard barely failed to make it on the governing board. The next year, the nominating committee heeded the warning and included Richard on their list of names.

Richard has had many sleepless nights since he began as an elder at the growing church. As the congregation burst at the seams, tensions rose. The session meetings turned out to be a series of ideas from the new younger members followed by scowls and head shaking from the older members. No one wanted to engage in a struggle, so the response of the larger body went quickly into placating the patriarchs, as the young leaders got brushed aside time and time again.

The pastoral staff overturned, new pastors took their places, and the expansion continued as they planned for a new sanctuary. With each decision the session had to make (chairs or pews, piano or organ, red or blue carpeting), the bitterness and grimaces increased. The original core of leadership had a stronghold on the power of the organization and the younger members were exhausted by the struggle. The meetings felt like a brutal game of "king of the mountain," in which the previous leadership stood with their feet securely planted on the peak of the hill ready to turn away any threat.

Many congregations long for intergenerational growth. Yet once it happens, they are rarely prepared for the stress that can also develop. Often churches do not realize that inviting young members into their congregation means allowing them to have some weight in decisions, and sharing power can be the largest obstacle in the way of ministering with young adults. And, as Ethan Watters notes, "Things that change precipitously from one generation to the next are usually greeted by the older generation as the death of everything good and right."[5] And all too often, younger generations find themselves in Richard's position, trying to navigate through change in the middle of a heated battle for the summit of some sand hill. But no one likes to fight on his volunteer time. So, young people end up simply walking downhill and resume their wandering in a different direction.

Mountain Climbing Team

Somehow, we have to move from playing king of the mountain and become a mountain climbing team. As we scale the rocks together, we look for those members who are not making it, come alongside of them, and offer encouragement and support.

I am washing the dishes in my kitchen and looking out the window at my daughter, Calla, playing with the next-door neighbor. I love it when my only child spends time with them, because there are three children ranging from thirteen years old to thirteen months old. Innes, their mother, is a genius, definitely the best mom on the block. She used to run a preschool for poor children in Azerbaijan, so she knows all the tricks and has the ability to discipline any child with the kindest words. As a result, all the children in the neighborhood hang out at her home.

"Could you help me with Sophie?" Innes coaxes my daughter, Calla, to hand her baby a shovel. "You're bigger than her, so she looks up to you, you know. She always likes to learn from the big girls."

As her pleasant voice continues, I think, "So, that's how she does it." I have watched in amazement as an entire team of competitive twelve-year-old soccer players happily stopped in the middle of their game so that baby Sophie could wander onto the backyard field. Instead of becoming angry, Sophie's older brother cheers her on: "Go, Sophie! Go Sophie! She's going to be a great player some day!"

I'm pleased that Innes teaches Calla her important part in the community. Even before kindergarten begins, Calla's beginning to look after people smaller than her and finding ways to help them. She's aware of what younger children need and is becoming sensitive to her influence on them, no doubt because of our neighbor's inspiration.

As I put the last dish away, I hope that Calla holds on to these lessons because they will continue to be important the farther away from the sand pile she gets. Throughout her life, she will need to encourage younger people and understand her influence on them. That's how leaders are developed. Leaders do not simply spring up, ready for action; they are formed over years, with the intentional care of older generations.

From Power Protection to the Mores of Mentors

What if retiring ministers and elders were to devote half of the energy that they currently spend on filling positions into finding and developing young leaders? What if they could make a commitment to eating lunch with a potential leader once a month? Might it not begin the process of strengthening our leadership and ameliorating the crisis? They could begin the long process of mentoring them by identifying their strengths and finding places where their talents could be developed in our local churches and our larger denominational bodies.

John Wimberly, the head of staff at Western Presbyterian Church, always looks for ways that he can develop young leadership. It grows out of his MBA training. He makes an important distinction between leaders and managers: leaders have dynamic vision that motivates people and changes things. Managers, on the other hand, make sure that things function, as they should, within the budget and in a timely manner. Leaders and managers are both important for an organizational structure, yet leaders become managers when they are in one place for an extended period of time. Their edge dulls and the company loses that important vision. So, top corporations have learned to identify and move leadership up as much as possible.

Lamenting that this practice was unusual in the church, John began to concentrate on developing leadership and a culture of mentoring young people has begun in the congregation. So, when so many denominational churches resigned themselves to saying goodbye to their young confirmation students, hoping that they will show back up for their first child's baptism, Western hired a campus minister to make sure that progressive young people are nurtured during these vital years of discernment.

As a staff and congregation, we encourage college members to become youth leaders and Sunday school teachers. The nominating committee actively looks for young men and women to serve as elders and deacons. This vital spiritual community constantly finds different ways to reach out to its student neighbors at George Washington University.

Ron Lehker, a Western member who just turned eighty years old, has a gift for relating to college students. As a retired school principal, he spent his life developing the best aspects of children, and his work continues today. Almost every student in our congregation knows Ron because of his actively engaged radar, which scans large groups of people, always on the lookout for young potential.

At Western, our staff relationship is a mentoring relationship, as I regularly talk through my mistakes and hopes and John guides me with his decades of experience. And during my time as a pastor at Western, I have been thrilled to have conversations with young, highly gifted women and men who are contemplating many careers, including ordained ministry. They have an exciting road ahead of them, and they will need all the support and encouragement they can get.

John's hope does not stop at the local church. Frustrated that our best young pastoral candidates were not being called to the finest churches, he began meeting with governing bodies to brainstorm what they could do about the situation. As John's retirement draws nearer, he gets more and more focused on equipping young leaders and making sure that they are in positions to thrive. I am grateful that I have been the recipient of his visionary advice.

Clergy

"We will not have younger generations in our congregations until we learn how to have young pastors leading our congregations," says Tara Spuhler McCabe, a thirty-two-year-old associate pastor of the historic New York Avenue Presbyterian Church. Tara has a strong administrative mind and is exceptional at seeing the needs and assets of large organizations. I nod my head in agreement, but it also comes as troubling news.

It seems that young clergy are getting harder and harder to find. The average age of seminarians beginning their studies in 1999 was just over thirty-five, and the average age of mainline Protestant clergy was fifty-one.[6] Of this trend toward older clergy, Martin E. Marty remarks, "the clergy are old and think old and don't last long, that does something to the spirit of the enterprise, commitment for the long haul, and maturation-in-office—all of which mean so much in many situations."[7]

The statistics seem to support Tara's conclusion. Jackson Carroll reports, "If one compares the average age of current U.S. church members with that of the clergy, one finds that they are quite similar: laity in most denominations averages in their mid-50s—much the same as their clergy."[8]

The young clergy who are in installed positions have a tendency to leave. As young pastors begin their calls, many times they get frustrated within a few years of ordination. In the Presbyterian Church (USA), we are currently in the midst of a clergy shortage: 43 percent of our pulpits do not have installed pastors because of the lack of church resources and human resources.[9] There is a constant stream of articles and letters to the editor in our denominational periodicals that question if this is a "crisis" or not. I am astonished that it could be considered anything but a catastrophe, when almost half of the denomination's congregations cannot call clergy.

We have difficulty retaining new clergy and, Carroll points out, in all traditions (including Catholic, Mainline Protestant, Conservative Protestant, and Historic Black), younger pastors are more likely to express doubt regarding their call to ministry. Almost half of the clergy under age forty-five doubt their call.[10]

When talking to young clergy, it seems that there are three reasons for their dissatisfaction: inadequate compensation, gender discrimination, and lack of power.

INADEQUATE COMPENSATION

First, there is the problem of money. One of the major reasons why young people do not enter the ministry is because they cannot afford to become pastors. Newly ordained pastors often get jobs in small congregations and associate positions in which they barely have the resources to survive. There is a link between small churches and leaving the ministry: low salaries. Carroll's research cites that the disparity of mainline pastors' salaries between small churches (under 100 members) and large churches (351 to 1,000 members) is sizeable, with small church pastors receiving a median salary (including housing) of $35,400 and large church pastors receiving $67,017.[11]

When Carroll related the dissatisfaction of clergy to certain aspects of ministry, inadequate compensation topped the list. In another recent study of Lutheran, United Methodist, Assembly of God, and Presbyterian pastors who left the ministry, financial difficulties were cited again.[12]

Some churches have the romantic notion that pastors should be like the lilies of the field, and never worry, especially about their compensation. There is no doubt that God will clothe us, but congregations must realize that God relies on them to do the necessary tailoring. If we do not get paid enough to buy a home and educate our children, we will be forced to find other ways to support ourselves and our families. Therefore, churches must begin to pay their ministers in accord with the real cost of living in the area in which the church is located. For congregations, it can be extremely difficult to keep up with the housing costs of a community, but the investment is absolutely necessary for the health of our communities and our denominations.

In most congregations, there must be an advocate for a pastor's pay, as the minister can rarely win a fight for her salary herself. When one young pastor on the expensive West Coast shared her real financial concerns with her personnel committee, in response she received a negative review with the statement, "It is unattractive for our minister to talk so much about money."

Yet, as the bills come due, it can be very unattractive indeed as financial burdens weigh down heavily on every aspect of a young pastor's life. That load becomes an even heavier sacrifice when carried by a single minister who would like to own a home. And for those who are married, the tensions of the pastorate do not seem worth it when they are compounded by financial pressures. The financial situation of most pastors can have a terrible effect on their home life; studies show that pastors who report financial stress also have family stress.[13]

Often churches cannot understand the financial pressures of pastors in their twenties and thirties. Far from being materialistic, most young ministers are simply trying to survive. One clergy couple in the United Church of Christ reported having this struggle when they were trying to decide if they should split a fulltime job. They had hefty student loans from graduate school, so they had to do some tough negotiations with the calling committee when they decided to receive a call on the East Coast. "We just didn't want to get to the church and then start resenting them because we couldn't make it financially. We knew that wouldn't be good for us or good for the ministry."

Yet, many young pastors do not have this foresight and find them-selves struggling in a position where they cannot make ends meet. It therefore makes sense that some young clergy will leave their call within a few years. For women, with their very slim hope for advancement, the call to leave the ministry is stronger, as they have little chance of making their situation better in the years to come.

I used to think that clergy who dropped out were not tough enough, or that they lacked some sort of spiritual stamina that a pastor needs—that they just didn't have the necessary tenacity to "make it." Now I understand that many of them made a wise choice: to provide for themselves and their families.

In a medium-sized mainline church in California, the congrega-tion conducted a pastoral search for an assistant minister and found a wonderful young candidate. She seemed perfect in every way, but the relationship crumbled when they negotiated her salary.

The senior pastor became furious when he saw that the amount she was asking for came very near his compensation. This senior pastor had served the church faithfully for twenty years, always receiving an annual two to three percent increase. After years of building the sea-side church, he was happy with his package until the church began the negotiations with the arriving pastor. Then he fumed, "Here comes my new assistant, fresh out of seminary, and she's asking for my salary!"

He wondered why this younger generation of ministers was so greedy and unwilling to make material sacrifices for the good of the church. He could not figure out why she could not serve for the amount for which he had happily worked for so many years.

What the senior pastor could not see was the college and seminary education debt that the new pastor carried into her position. Plus, the cost of real estate had increased substantially since the older minister had been installed in his position. Since he owned a home in the area, the increase was a wonderful boost for his net worth as he looked toward retirement, but it meant that the next generation of pastors would need much more income to buy a house.

With the rising expenses of education and housing, it costs more for younger clergy to live and the wages in our churches have not kept up with the financial demands of our society. Many seasoned ministers have received an annual increase of two to three percent, but those small increments do not translate into a secure living when a person enters the real estate market. And the strain becomes even more difficult when churches expect assistant pastors to work for half the earnings of their senior colleagues.

Pastors get frustrated because young associates ask for nearly the same salary as the head of staff, and small churches stagger under the wages that new ministers hope to make. Unless they take realistic account of their housing and education costs, church members can easily see young ministers as greedy. In the Presbyterian Church (USA), those clergy who took out student loans in seminary accrued an average of $32,959 of debt, and that does not even include their undergraduate loans, spouse's liabilities, car payment, or credit card debt.

The United Church of Christ has begun to understand what effects these financial obligations can have on their churches. "The educational debt faced by many seminary graduates represents not only individual hardship but theological crisis," the General Synod declared as they worked toward solutions to alleviate the problem.[14]

Young clergy find themselves in difficult financial circumstances when they enter parish ministry, and even more strained when they think about buying a home, saving for retirement, and sending their own children to college.[15] They are not going into the profession to make a lot of money, but they do have to make enough to pay the bills and live. Many pastors in their twenties and thirties begin their careers in a hole of debt that older ministers, deacons, and elders cannot imagine, and crawling out of that chasm is very difficult to accomplish as a pastor in a small church, where many young male clergy begin their career, and where most women stay throughout their career.

I have also been surprised to realize that even when a church grows exponentially, the pastor's salary still often does not advance more that two to three percent. I am not advocating that a minister's salary should be tied to the number on the membership rolls, but it seems that congregations might want to consider how pay increases could positively affect the longevity of the pastor's career, especially if that minister's presence has substantially encouraged the church's income.

GENDER DISCRIMINATION

For women, the trend of leaving pastoral ministry is more pronounced. After seminary, women are less likely to enter parish ministry, and by the third job, 37 percent of women enter either a non-parish ministry position or secular work, in comparison to 26 percent of men.[16]

Even though women make up over half of our seminary students and have excelled academically, clergywomen are much less likely to move up to large church positions. In the Presbyterian Church (USA), 94 percent of women cite "discrimination in the call process" as an issue.[17] In 1998, the position of women clergy was clear in all mainline denominations: 28 percent of female clergy were serving as assistant or associate pastors compared to 11 percent of male clergy. As the *New York Times* reports, for the first ten years after ordination, men and women hold similar positions. Yet in their second decade, 70 percent of men have moved on to medium-sized and large congregations compared to only 37 percent of women. Women account for only three percent of pastors who lead large mainline Protestant churches.[18]

Sometimes churches hire women because they can get a bargain; they know that an experienced woman will be less expensive than a man. In a Presbyterian Church (USA) survey, 85 percent of women cited "negotiating equitable terms of call" as an issue.[19]

The general morale of women clergy in our congregations has hit despairing depths. Behind closed doors, when there's a safe space for them to speak, many women feel cynical, angry, and desperate. Some women who try to send their children to college and look toward retirement resent the fact that they worked so hard, for so many years, with so little pay. After decades of experience, these gifted women still have a difficult time moving up in this climate of discrimination. Younger women see their struggles and pray that things will change, but they become agitated by the slow progress.

One thirty-eight-year-old female assistant pastor, whose congregation will be searching for a head of staff, disclosed, "I'm entering my tenth year of ministry, and I recognize that my congregation will probably hire a male senior pastor, who has the same credentials that I do, and pay him $50,000 more than they pay me. How can I keep working in this environment for the next 30 years?"

In the years to come, it will be absolutely vital for larger churches to start hiring female heads of staff. Women either move up or they move out. With our current practices, the church cuts off the potential and rejects half of its clergy by disregarding women candidates. Young women who begin as pastors learn quickly that they will never be able to break through that thick stained glass ceiling. And many women, after exhausting small church and associate positions, feel a call to a head of staff position, but they become jaded after long searches lead to disappointment and start looking for jobs beyond the church.

A clergywoman's confidence plummets when she sees churches pass over her experienced colleagues time and time again. Large churches must realize that their decisions as they choose their head of staff will not just make an impact on who stands in their pulpit for the next few years; it affects every congregation in the nation. Sizeable churches have the power to turn around decades of injustice and lift the morale for generations to come. Now that many qualified women are poised to move into larger pulpits, this appalling discrimination can finally come to an end.

Lack of Authority

When I ask other young pastors why they would leave the ministry, they speak of a general lack of respect and power that seems all too common. As soon as I broach the subject, the stories pour out:

"I sit in a meeting, and no one listens to me."

"When I try to do basic administrative work, I get feedback that I'm a control freak."

"They hired me to redevelop this church, but they never want to hear anything I have to say."

"None of my [young] friends can stay in their positions for more than two to three years. It's because they have no authority in their church. They're stuck with all this stuff to do, and all of the complaints, but they have no power."

"When my older colleague preaches, the congregation tells him, 'Good sermon.' Whenever I preach, they tell me 'Your hair looks great today!' The head of staff has never gotten a compliment on his hair!"

"I get sexually harassed by old men in my church. When I complain about it, I'm told that I should just ignore it."

"I read books that tell me it's going to take at least five years before people start to trust the pastor in a small church. That just sounds excruciating."

"I have often been in situations where I have a high level of responsibility and a heavy workload, but inadequate resources and authority
(not to mention compensation) to accomplish the task at hand. It's
frustrating and hard not to feel bitter when your gifts are recognized,
but exploited."

"After seven years as an associate, the senior pastor and personnel committee completely changed my job description without even
discussing it with me. They just presented my new job at the congregational meeting."

"I am a pastor, doctoral student, and father of two. At a recent
academic/ professional society meeting, I was repeatedly addressed
as 'young man' and asked by a stranger to 'run around' and set up the
room for a seminar I was attending. Later, in a line for a plenary session,
I watched as the older people in front of me were greeted pleasantly by
the usher; the same usher warned me sternly to take only one resource
packet for the event. The next day I overheard someone lamenting the
lack of younger people in the society. Go figure."

Tom began his second pastorate at the age of thirty when a small
congregation hired him to revitalize their church. As he began the job,
Tom was excited about the possibilities, but the congregation quickly
restrained him. He maintained a traditional worship style and his hymn
selections came out of the denomination's book, but the service always
included a spiritual or some international music, which many parishioners complained about. He tried to rebuff the comments by saying,
"Oh, it can't be that bad. It's just a couple of minutes each week."

In meetings, church leadership rejected Tom's ideas and continued
to ask the former retired minister for advice. They called the previous
pastor out of retirement each time someone got married or was in the
hospital. Anytime Tom would step up to coordinate something in the
church, he would receive feedback that he was "too controlling," and
making too many "unilateral decisions." Like Alice in Wonderland, he
felt trapped in a shrinking house by the confining church leadership.
Soon Tom's position became so small that he could not find any space
to be a leader. In fact, he had so little power that he was not even able
to complete minimal job duties.

The young minister began to scour books on family systems theo-
ries and shepherding small churches. He read that he needed to be in

the church for a decade before people began to listen to him, but he saw the church declining fast and knew that he did not have ten years to wait before he could begin to do his job. He tried desperately to become a better leader and was frustrated by his inability to be able to salvage the sinking ship.

He found it impossible to get guidance from leaders in the denomination who seemed preoccupied with managing disputes regarding the church's position on sexuality and trying to keep the largest and most conservative churches happy. So he finally left the church, feeling powerless, defeated, and unsupported. His is not an unusual story.

Contexts of Sharing Leadership

Pastoring a small church often means that the minister serves in isolation, with little encouragement from denominational staff or connection with other clergy. Most of the time, the minister doesn't have sufficient financial resources. Many young clergy have been stranded in solo positions, leading our most difficult congregations with no assistance or even recognition for what they do. The time in our denominational meetings are filled with retirement celebrations (for people who often do not actually retire), but there is very little voice given to the young small church pastor.

In order to encourage young pastors and to alleviate the clergy dropout rate, perhaps we can make small church positions better work environments through congregational, governing body, and clergy support.

CONGREGATION

I asked Ellen Babinsky, a church history professor, why people leave the parish. She had a unique perspective: as the dean of students, she gets to know many seminarians on a personal level and keeps in touch with many of them after they graduate. She worked as a parish associate in a local congregation, was actively involved with governing bodies, and had herself left the pastorate to become a seminary professor. After a short pause, she answered, "Well, I'm sure most of it has to do with all the criticism pastors have to endure. I can't believe the amount of complaints that pastors get. Even when a pastor loves her job, I wonder how long it's going to last when there are so many complaints. You know, a person can only work on fumes for so long."

At the very least, we can begin improving the positions by cutting out the overwhelming criticism. One member of a congregation told me, "In my family, we used to go to church on Sunday morning, and on Sunday afternoon, we would have the pastor for lunch!"—meaning that his family would pick apart everything that the pastor had done or said that morning. With cutting, biting complaints, they consumed the young man along with their chicken.

I have been told that accepting criticism is just a part of the job as a pastor, and certainly in any leadership position there will be complaints. But let us consider the damage that continual attacks cause. It's terribly painful to watch when a caring, considerate pastor becomes the brunt of verbal condemnation. The bitter comments that some congregations heap on their ministers can discourage the most hopeful young pastors. In a small congregation, every grievance eventually funnels back to the pastor. Everything. In fact, the minister usually hears one criticism about five times: the nasty remarks during the women's Bible study, the protest against her two percent increase, the grumbling about his preaching style. The comments are rarely made anonymously; they typically come like a knife in the back with an address label attached.

There are times when real grievances need to be made and there should be appropriate avenues of accountability, especially when allegations of ethical misconduct arise. But if a member has some words of advice for his pastor, he should go to her directly. Face-to-face communication allows the member to choose words wisely, and it keeps flippant criticisms from echoing down the hall into the pastor's study.

Also, before a church member objects to her pastor because she did not like the way he tore the bread during communion or because she didn't wear a string of pearls with her suit, the member can remind herself that there is a clergy shortage, and in this crucial time, small churches are most affected.

If you are a member of a small congregation and you have an installed pastor, realize what a wonderful and rare gift that is. Appreciate your minister and look for ways to encourage her or him. If you cannot bring yourself to do this, then at least follow the words of that old adage, "if you can't say anything nice, then just don't say anything at all."

Katherine, a young pastor in the South, left her congregation after three years of constant complaints and a seething evaluation of her performance. In spite of the criticism, it was a growing church. New programs sprang up and there was more vitality than that congregation had seen for years.

The church didn't realize that Katherine received two or three phone calls every week from other congregations, asking her to consider being their pastor. So, they kept complaining about her: she wore the wrong clothes, her voice was too screechy, she was not a strong enough leader, she was too strong of a leader, she was too young, she was too aggressive, and the church had never really wanted a woman pastor in the first place. Katherine laughed off the petty comments, then ignored them, then caringly confronted them, and then willed herself to grow thicker skin. Nothing seemed to work. The complaints kept pouring in and Katherine grew weary and stressed.

After a great deal of prayer and counseling, Katherine finally realized that she could no longer take the harsh work environment and took a position at another congregation. When she circulated her letter of resignation, the members of her church were completely shocked, because to them things appeared to be going so well.

In her exit interview, she cited the environment of criticism as her main reason for leaving. The personnel committee responded, "What? The members of the church didn't mean to make you leave with those complaints. They just wanted to control you." Katherine is now happily serving another congregation. Her former church has yet to find another pastor.

As I look back on my ministry, I am thankful for the gifts that my first congregation gave to me. I fell in love with First Presbyterian Church of Abbeville because of its rich Cajun culture. Everyone there seemed to be cooking or dancing all the time. The church potlucks were not just meager casseroles; they were made up of some of the finest food I have ever tasted. The white slat-board church stood proud, close to the middle of the town square in Abbeville. The foundation was not firm; in fact, like many structures in the swamps of Louisiana, it was built on stilts to withstand flooding and hurricanes. In places, I could look through the wooden floor boards and see the grass growing beneath me. The Christian education building (which was a retired Army barracks), sagged in a few corners and the pipes regularly froze.

The church did not have the resources to attract a pastor who would stay for a long time; instead, they saw themselves as a training ground for young ministers, an outpost after seminary. The older members looked back on their extensive history and pointed to the long-standing pastors in our denomination who began their ministry in that church. While the tenure of their pastors was often short, they took great pride in the person's longevity in the ministry. While some ministers leave after their first call, those who began their careers in Abbeville usually retired as pastors. The congregation took chances on young clergy and was the first church in their community to hire a woman pastor. In short, they had a level of comfort with taking risks, because they saw themselves as mentors, a teaching church for inexperienced ministers.

I was twenty-six years old when I was called to First Presbyterian Church of Abbeville. During the congregational vote, a positive discussion ensued. In the end, the vote was unanimous; the membership realized that just as they all went to doctors who were younger than they were, so it made sense to hire a spiritual leader who was younger. Plus, the organist added, "Youth attracts youth."

With this attitude, they could foster fine leadership within those walls. I left the congregation, with sadness and gratitude, because the congregation had taught me so much. Like many rural churches, we had the difficulties that come in small packages: most of the membership and leadership originated from one family, budgetary strain was exasperated by an insistence to "never touch the memorial money," and the buildings were in constant need of repair. However, the church allowed me a great deal of creativity during worship, welcoming narrative preaching and painting during the Sunday morning service, and the incorporation of different styles of music. They even encouraged our unorthodox youth choir.

When my daughter was born, I could not have asked for a more family-friendly work environment. The church literally embraced her with open arms and made it easy for me to balance the demands of my pastorate and home. With their care, I was strengthened, and so were they.

As small churches look for pastors, they want strong leaders who will help them grow, but with dwindling resources, they may have difficulty attracting and keeping experienced clergy. Yet, the model that Abbeville developed may help. If small churches could begin to see themselves as a training ground, with the important work of nurturing leaders, then they may take more chances on clergy early on in their careers and allow more creativity and mistakes. When small churches have the vision to develop leadership, they might see that they are the key to our entire denomination's thriving.

In the church's search process as they look for pastoral leadership, small churches could be taught their essential role to nurture the pastor as the pastor nurtures the congregation. They are not "just a small church;" they make up a close to half of our congregations. Churches have an important part in developing young ministers, giving ministers a chance to foster their creative gifts, and encouraging pastors to continue in their calling. Small congregations need to realize their piece in the bigger puzzle: they are the key to clergy shortage. If they can cultivate supportive environments for men and women, then they will have a much healthier church, and we will all have much stronger denominations.

GOVERNING BODY

I could not have stayed in the Abbeville church for the full three years if my husband and I had not had support from a local governing body. Richard Brownlee and Judy Gabel Roeling, the General Presbyter and Associate Presbyter, took great care in shaping us as leaders. The governing body informed us about subsidized continuing education events, nominated us for important leadership positions, paid for pulpit supply during my maternity leave, and granted my congregation strategic revitalization money that helped pay for increases in my salary.

We could alleviate stress on new pastors across the board with a similar shift of emphasis in our denominations. Governing bodies are reluctant to pour money into dwindling congregations, since they assume that resources can better be used by beginning new church developments. Denominational leadership puts little energy into small congregations because larger churches are seen as much more important in the administrative structure. Yet, when we let our small churches languish, our young leadership suffers too.

Instead of seeing smaller churches as fallow ground waiting to dry up, we can envision these churches as the important soil in which the seeds of great ministry develop and where wonderful, full-fledged service takes place. If we ignore our small churches, we disregard our denominations' rich training ground. Instead of placing young pastors into these settings with few financial, social, and educational resources, how about including them in the vital work of mentoring ministers? Instead of governing denominational bodies giving charity to keep struggling churches stay open for one more year, they could begin offering grants to ministers for their enrichment and guidance.

In our current structures, we have a proliferation of entry-level pastorates. In other words, most of our positions do not require much experience and a pastor could find himself in a solo or associate position for his entire career. So, if we want to retain pastors, challenge them, and encourage professional growth, we can find ways to compensate them for additional experience and education.

Of course, the budgets of many mainline governing bodies have been dwindling, so it's easier to recommend such an investment than to allocate the resources. Perhaps the money is not there—yet. But if we begin to see nurturing young leaders as a top priority, the resources will often follow.

For instance, our local governing body recently passed two motions: (1) they spent $29 million for building a camp and (2) they raised the minimum salary requirement. Both motions passed. With a little bit of debate, they happily handed over millions for the retreat center (while incurring possible debt for the larger body), but laypeople and clergy were confounded by the minimum salary requirement. "I just don't know where we're going to get the money," concerned parishioners and pastors whispered to each other, not realizing that a shift in priorities would have paid for the cost of cultivating leaders: the interest generated from the camp money could have nurtured young pastoral leadership and provided for housing assistance for generations to come.

With our current practices, our denominations look like a giant octopus with a withering head. The pastoral leadership, which is central to vital denominations, is drying up. Our churches need pastors, and for those leaders to become restored, pastors need kind, supportive work environments.

CLERGY SUPPORT

The isolation that pastors experience reminds me of that feeling of being lonely at a party. Uncomfortably shaking the ice in our cups, we are surrounded by people, but we can't find anyone with whom we can talk. We have worries, fears, hopes, and dreams that are not always appropriate to share with our congregation. Also, we realize that the bond with our members should (for the most part) end with that particular position.

It would have been this way for me in Abbeville, except there were a few culturally diverse pastors who immediately invited me to their lectionary group. Each Tuesday afternoon, I drove out to Jeanerette, kept going straight after the sugar cane processing plant, through the downtown and LeJeune's Bakery (where one can buy the best French bread in the United States), and turned right into the nest of the neighborhood houses. Then, across the railroad tracks, there was a wonderful United Methodist Church, where Fulton Raymond ministered for decades. The "United" in the title was extremely important to Fulton, because it meant that the segregation had ended in the denomination, and he continued to fight stridently for unity.

We met together on Tuesday afternoon in the dark, wood-paneled fellowship hall to discuss the group of passages for the next Sunday. If we were lucky, Fulton's wife would make an amazing meatloaf that had cheese and jalapeños rolled in the center of it. But most of the time, we would gather around a cup of thick chicory coffee.

Purcell Church and Fulton Raymond, a couple of retired African American pastors, quickly began telling me what I should and should not be doing in my parish. Coming home from those first meetings, I was annoyed that they were patronizing me just because I was young and fresh out of seminary. However, I quickly realized that these men were mentoring me. In that particular culture, African Americans have a strong system of building up new leaders in their community, and I became an extremely grateful recipient of their wisdom.

When I came in carrying worries about a church argument, Purcell would survey the situation and respond thoughtfully, "I wouldn't take sides on this one." Or during my first year, when the beginning ministers were looking for a fresh, new way to present the Easter story, Fulton looked at us like our heads had just fallen off and proceeded to give us the most valuable Holy Day preaching advice, "Fresh? New? Just give them the story. For a lot of people, the only time they come to church is to hear this story, and you better give them this story."

Week after week, the pastors met with me. Not because they needed my insight on the lectionary passage, but because they had a keen awareness of how much I needed their counsel. They understood their calling as mentors and invested crucial time into forming another generation of Episcopal, Presbyterian, and Methodist pastors. Their sense of responsibility was broader than obtaining and keeping power in the United Methodist Church; instead, they looked at the entire sandbox of their community and recognized that their years of experience could help form, shape, and grow strong leaders.

Instead of playing king of the mountain with us, we became a mountain climbing team, as Purcell and Fulton navigated the rough terrain of those first years with us. With their many years on the top of the mountain, they had a great vantage point. They could see the danger spots and often predicted where we might slip. They understood that even the sturdiest community leaders would have a tough time traversing the trail alone the first time. So they came alongside us, listening carefully and advising when needed, and I was always grateful for their support.

As pastors, we do well to learn how to care for one another, giving sought-after advice, or just acting as a sounding board and offering some encouragement. When I met with a gathering of female clergy throughout our region, we sat in a large intergenerational circle, filled with unbelievable collective wisdom. We were asked to introduce ourselves, and after the name and position, the younger women kept adding another piece of information: "I see the experience in this room, and it makes me really wish that I had a mentor, someone who's been through this before and can guide me in what to do."

Churches are notorious for their "good old boys' network," which can work against women and people of color, but sitting in that room made me wonder if we could begin a more inclusive model of mentoring. Perhaps we could extend the vision and wisdom of older generations so that they might learn to leave an inheritance to the church. Then, with guiding care, young leadership of all types can flourish.

Reflection Questions

1. What traditions does your congregation have that support your pastor? In what ways do you show your appreciation?
2. Imagine what you would want for your pastor (education, home, retirement savings, education for her or his children). Could a new pastor buy an adequate house in the locale of the church with the compensation package that your church provides? Could she or he support a family on the salary? If you have an experienced pastor, is she or he making above the income that a new pastor would need? What steps can your congregation take to make up the difference?
3. How could denominations be more encouraging to young pastors? Is there any room for reallocating assets so that ministers could afford a home? Is there any vision in your denomination for repaying the student loans for clergy?
4. How can you mentor or encourage another pastor or layperson?
5. How can we begin encouraging the leadership of young adults in our churches? Are there any visible leadership positions into which your church can be encouraging young adults to step?

CHAPTER 7

Nurturing
Spiritual
Community

I'm traveling to Austin, Texas, and the cheapest way to fly is to go through Houston. Unfortunately, a deluge of storms bombards Texas on my way, and we have a terrible time resuming the second half of the journey. To make matters worse, instead of postponing the flight and dealing with all of the headaches of rescheduling, the airline herds us onto the plane, moves us away from the gate onto an unused corner of the tarmac, and makes us wait—for three hours in anticipation of a twenty minute flight. The airport is completely closed down, and we're held captive in this fretfully small space.

I've traveled a lot on airplanes. Since I was a teenager, I looked for any opportunity that I could find to explore. In all of those years, I never liked airplane chitchat much. I like to sleep on flights, so I avoid eye contact with the person next to me because it may be possible that I could spend the next hours trapped in a confining space and a confining conversation. But I notice something different this time. The nature of airline travel changed drastically, and it's not just because the seats are closer together. It's because everyone has a cell phone.

The mobiles are affecting the community on this flight. Instead of turning to her neighbor in seat 23B and groaning about the extra hours on the tarmac, each person calls the friend who will pick her up and complains about it. After they finish with that conversation, they call another person and another.

No one talks to their neighbor on the plane.

I may only notice this trend because I accidentally packed my phone in my suitcase and don't have it with me. So, I anxiously sit and listen to everyone else grumbling to their friends, spouses, and children. I want to grouse to someone, so I give up my usual ban on talking to the person next to me, and begin to engage him in a conversation, only to have him avoid eye contact and lift his index finger at me. I see that he has a tiny cell device in his other ear and I'm interrupting his call.

I mumble an apology, but it doesn't matter. He isn't listening anyway.

It's a little sad, in a way, and I wonder if what's happening on my flight is a microcosm of what happens for many of us, especially young adults. For younger generations, the computer has become an extension of who we are. Facebook and blogs account for our virtual community and keep us communicating with our friends who live far away. The Internet has been a wonderful gift to a wandering generation. I frequently hear from people from my past, even classmates from sixth grade, who googled my name out of curiosity. People carry BlackBerry's around so they can stay in constant touch with others.

I have gotten to know people over e-mail in deep and meaningful ways. As a pastor in the District of Columbia, I keep in contact with our parishioners through my office keyboard, and I am always surprised at how personal concerns easily flow through e-mail (especially when they are written late at night), and I wonder if the same worries would ever arise in face-to-face settings. Our capacity for conveying emotion through the Internet is so strong that loving marriages even originate in cyberspace.

Yet something's not working. There is something lifeless and colorless about our existence. More and more, people enter my office, telling me, "I just don't know where I can meet people. I've tried everything. I just want to meet someone." They have tried Internet dating and mustering up love in a nightclub, but to no avail. And it's not just romantic relationships that are difficult to develop. Friendships are hard too. Young adults move so often, from job to job, apartment to apartment, and state to state, that they have difficulty forming community. With their ability to keep technological bonds with their past, sometimes they neglect to form physical and spiritual bonds in their present moment.

Yet in our congregations, we have a great opportunity to make a change, to form communities, and become places where people can meet each other. We can develop nurturing relationships, connecting with one another as the body of Christ.

From Committees to Community

In church, we often build community through committee work, which is curious, because attending committee meetings is my least favorite part about being a pastor.[1] I respect committee work, because in a healthy, functioning system, it is a democratic way of getting things done and allows the inclusion of a wide range of people in decision making. The structure allows the labor of the church to be dispersed. Committees let more people take ownership and responsibility for the work of our congregations. But (if they include the young members of the church) they often take place in the exhaustion of the evening or on Sunday afternoon, when many people are hungry for lunch and some rest.

In one church, the pastor tried hard to make the business meetings of the church into spiritual communities. It was an ambitious idea and the congregation certainly needed a space to form a connection with God and one another, so they began each meeting with prayer and Bible study. Unfortunately, this didn't enhance the sense of friendship among the members or deepen their spiritual lives; it just made each meeting an hour longer, so the members left the gatherings frustrated, tired, and hungry.

Committee work can become wearisome. The best of people comes out in those point-by-point agenda discussions, but the worst of them can come out too. Often, as we gather in cold metal folding chairs, we get to know the dysfunctions of each person without any background information. We quickly find out that many people have a personal agenda barely hidden underneath the official agenda. A person who has great passion and love for the church can quickly become cynical and jaded after sitting through meetings.

We look around the room and we can describe each personality. There is the person who volunteers for every task and never gets any of them completed; the one who argues against every motion until each action stalls for months; the man who never wants to spend any money and scrutinizes each penny in the income and expenditure lines; the woman who can foresee every facility disaster and wants to replace everything (the roof, boiler, air conditioner, pipes, and electrical wiring) immediately. There are the program nay-sayers, social justice visionaries, narcissists, and caregivers. Some people have a new idea every week, while others highly resist the very notion of change.

We rely on meetings to get things done, and an artful leader keeps each personality in check, encouraging some voices to speak and moderating others. The chair makes sure that the body passes motions in good order, remains open to the movement of the Spirit, and maintains an efficient schedule. In our committees, we gather to pray for the vision of the church, to remember our mission, to seek God's guidance, and get business completed. Sometimes we build relationships as a byproduct of our administrative meetings; yet, it can be a mistake when we rely solely on committees as the central format in which we build community. Instead, we do well to begin an intentional process of nurturing an incarnational ministry of presence through preaching, testimony, and prayer.

Incarnational Ministry

As churches become more and more hospitable to younger generations, we will need to stop relying on administrative committees to make our spiritual and social connections; instead, let us encourage incarnational tribes and communities. While understanding the importance of our bodies being present, we can venture beyond our flat black and white texts and engage all of our senses: sight, sound, touch, smell, and taste.

As Christians, we are people of the living word. We believe that the law, poetry, and prophecies form our communities, and those words were embodied by the flesh and blood of Jesus Christ. And since Jesus's time, we have built the body of Christ out of our own imperfect parts.

We have become his feet, hands, mouths, arms, and legs as we care for one another and the world.

As we make up this body, there is something important in our own physical selves, as we learn to be present with one another, seeing the steady gaze of a person's eyes, hearing the sound of a resonant voice, feeling the warmth of another's hands, smelling the aroma that fills the air, and then tasting the food that we consume.

ATTACHED COMMUNITIES

We can see this incarnational idea at work in the way that younger generations raise their children. The ideal manner in which sons and daughters are nurtured has changed dramatically as attachment parenting has become the predominant approach to raising kids and many have traded in their Dr. Spock books for those of the Drs. Sears.

Physical touch has become extremely important in raising children. In the attachment parenting approach, fathers and mothers strive to encourage healthy emotional and physical bonds with their infants in the hope that they will become secure adults. In the earliest days, those connections flourish with breastfeeding, holding, and sleeping with a child. Now dads can be found in the grocery store with slings around their necks, their babies nestled at their bellies, comforted by their dads' breath, movement, and speech.

Many moms and dads have traded in the formula for the breast, the playpen for the sling, and the crib for the family bed. Parents learn to attend more to high-need children and soothe temper tantrums with increased communication. Young adults form their children through positive reinforcement, time outs, and kind words.

Young parents often endure criticism for this from older generations who insist they are spoiling their children and making them the center of everything. But the intended goal of this time-intensive manner of parenting is that children might feel comfort and security; that sons and daughters will know that their cries of hunger or loneliness will be met with milk and a loving touch; and that they might learn caring, responsive behavior from their parents.

A detriment of this concentrated care for children is that young parents can tend to the needs of their children so much that they forget to take care of themselves. The family bed can cause sleepless nights and decreased intimacy with a spouse. The demands of endless breastfeeding can be exhausting, especially for a working mom who has to pump on her lunch break in a metal bathroom stall. Yet, generally speaking, the ideals of attachment parenting portray what moms and dads long for when they raise their children: loving, responsive bonds of intimacy within a caring family. Through their parenting choices, young adults try to create a just social order that tends to the emotional and physical needs of each person.

Jesse Quam is a 36-year-old licensed clinical social worker who has worked with teenagers in a therapeutic wilderness setting for ten years. Throughout his experience, he has seen how important it is for families to create healthy attachments. "I can have a beautiful rose," Jesse says, "but if I keep it in the basement, in the dark, it will die. It has to be outside. It has to have sun and be in an environment to grow. It's the same with people: They need to be in supportive environments, they need to be less isolated and in safe places, they need to be attached to a community and to the land."

Jesse strives to create a supportive environment with his infant daughter, Elsa. "Elsa can tell when I'm stressed. She knows it on a physical level. When she's upset, I can sit with her, look into her eyes, and she calms down. She knows that I'm fully present with her."

He expands on the importance of parents being near their children when he talks about his work: "When teenagers are at-risk, we [therapists] look at their environment for clues. We talk to the parents who are working until eight or nine every night, and explain that they need to make lifestyle changes in order to nurture their children. It's important for them to be present with their family. Kids and adults need grounding time with each other."

As we continued our conversation, I realized that Jesse's use of the word "ground" and "environment" is intentional. In his therapeutic work, he understands that deep healing comes from attachment to a community and to the land. In Utah and North Carolina, he has worked in beautiful places and has found that the earth becomes a place of wholeness.

Jesse lowers his voice in concern as we talk about our generation. "We move around so much, and most of us have to live in urban settings. We become isolated from our communities. We lose our attachment to the land. We see it in our abuse of the earth—we pave over it, we litter it—because we've lost our connection with it. As a result, our environment becomes toxic and we don't make the necessary lifestyle changes to preserve it."

The church is in a unique position in our society to form spiritual communities, to restore this connection with God, each other, and the world. As we learn to live as members of the body of Jesus Christ, we begin to understand the richness of friendships, the holiness of community, and the hallowedness of our ground.

Hospitable Communities

Brian Merritt, my husband and a 37-year-old pastor at the Palisades Community Church, understands the importance of the incarnational aspects of ministry. When the small church first called him as their minister, he gave me a tour of the facilities. We stood in the lovely white sanctuary, walked down the red carpet runner, and admired the simple windows. The worship space was just the right size for his congregation, and could even handle more growth.

Down the hall were wonderful preschool classrooms, and even though the rooms were empty, the fresh artwork made them alive with the energy of children. But the thing that Brian got most excited about was at the bottom of another set of stairs. It was the generous, well-stocked kitchen, with an industrial range and a convection oven.

I didn't understand why this was so important to him until a few months later when I realized that he fashioned his ministry around hospitality. Palisades is a neighborhood church. They do not have much of a parking lot, but it doesn't matter because on Sunday mornings most people walk to the church.

As a central act of welcome, Brian joins with members of his church to bake bread. The youngest and oldest people of the congregation gather in the kitchen. They have tried dozens of recipes in their quest for the perfect loaf, from dark molasses bread to basic white. As Brian kneads the ingredients for the recommended fifteen minutes, he imagines and prays for the new people in his community. He remembers what it feels like to be moving, disorganized, and alienated.

He recalls how the deacons of First Presbyterian Church left a loaf of bread that welcomed us to Lincoln, Nebraska, and invited us to join their congregation over a decade ago. Then with enough flour and massaging, the clammy mixture becomes a warm, smooth, and perfectly blended ball of dough.

After letting it rise, the kitchen crew punches it, forms it, bakes it, and smells it. Brian explains that the scent is the prize, "When the church fills with the smell of bread, it makes you feel really good. People gather in the kitchen, just so they can smell it. Somehow, the warmth generates conversations among the members. We talk about the past and think about the future."

When the bread is baked, they knock gently on the bottom of the hard crust, listening for that hollow sound. Then, the congregation uses it for communion on Sunday morning, and Brian delivers it to the new residents of the neighborhood during the week. "People are rarely home, but I leave it at their door with a note. I often get e-mails thanking me for the welcome, and sometimes we get people who visit the church because of it."

It's a time-intensive project. It usually takes his entire Monday morning, but Brian says that it's always worth the effort because the community that begins in that kitchen extends to the Palisades neighborhood in a way that embodies all the senses.

Conversing Communities

With instant messages and e-mail, younger generations have learned to be concise, witty, and blunt. We can repeat soundbites with ease. But many people crave to have the time and space to draw out a story, to be able to tell the strange and wonderful ways that God has worked in their lives. Often, we cannot detect any purpose for our character building experiences until we take time to reflect, trace the events, and fashion a story out of them. The words form us even as we form them. The meaning flows, slowly, out from us.

There is power in a story. We know this, as followers of Jesus, who often answered difficult questions with the words, "There once was a man who...." His abiding parables have molded and shaped our worshiping communities for thousands of years. They order our lives, as we think of Caesar on one side of the coin; they teach us how to care for one another, as we remember the example of the Good Samaritan; and we cling to them in our times of crisis, as we pray to the Good Shepherd on our death beds.

The testimonies of people we know can move us in dramatic ways, and the stories that fill our pews can shape an entire community. Even a short admission can change the dynamics of a group. In a women's meeting that a thirty-four-year-old minister, MaryAnn McKibben Dana, attended, one mother confessed, "I have not done the dishes from yesterday's breakfast." MaryAnn noticed that with that admission, the atmosphere in the room changed completely. Everyone sighed, letting out their tension. Then they began taking in deep, full breaths of relief. Because one woman had told the truth, all of them relaxed.

At Western Presbyterian, we begin our new member classes sitting at three round tables. After dinner, we simply ask one another, "Tell us about your spiritual journey." The church is a caring place; in fact, I rarely hear unkind words about other members, so the trust level is quite high among the congregation. This healthy environment allows for a certain amount of vulnerability and honest exchange.

John, the head of staff, and I go first; we explain our family histories, our struggles with our faith, and our meandering call process. I am always moved by the stories that unfold next. Some have only a few words to say, and others could write many books with their depth and experience. Within these small groups, I have been touched by the sacred narratives of each person who enters the church.

In Washington, D.C., a person typically introduces herself with her title or position, but on this night, if the person's occupation makes it into the storyline, it is usually a peripheral mention. The heart of the account is how God speaks to each one of us. Each testimony forms our worshiping community anew.

Preaching: Which Side of the Hermeneutical Bridge are You On?

A couple of months ago, a few college students from the church came over for burritos and chips. Most of them were seniors and from different traditions; they were Lutheran, Methodist and Charismatic. So

I asked them, "Why did you start attending Western Presbyterian Church?"

Sarah Gillespie, a tall, bright woman, tucked her red hair behind her ear and responded, "I go there because the sermons mean something. They have to do with what we study and how we live."

For pastors, the most important thing that we do happens on Sunday morning: the sacraments, liturgy, prayers and Scripture readings feed us in this central tradition. In worship, we have a chance to do those things that our hearts crave to do all week. It is the one place that we have to opportunity to sing, to sit in silence, to confess what we have done wrong, and participate in the sacraments. Also, it's the one space where we can hear the oral tradition of preaching.

The demands of the pastorate seem to increase as the job description gets longer and longer. Young parents consistently lobby for more programs for their children. Aging Baby Boomers will require more palliative care. When a pastor's blocks of time get crowded, and she feels haunted by a hundred other things that she ought to be doing, the hours and energy for sermon preparation can still be strongly nurtured and protected by the minister and the congregation.

The craft of constructing a sermon is an amazing thing, but it cannot happen between noon and three p.m. on Saturday. Churches do well to support their pastors with adequate space for discernment and the formation of sermons, because the preparation takes great care.

As a pastor moves into the pulpit, she allows a few real moments for people to discern the Word of God. In this day and age, when live television is prerecorded and "reality" shows are carefully produced, we have fifteen minutes (more or less) each Sunday morning to unfurl this important oral art form. It is rare in our culture for a person to stand and speak before a crowd, without the momentary delay, production, and editing that television and documentaries provide. In this form of preaching, ministers usually speak without many visual distractions; we allow people to soak up stories and listen to Scriptures.

Preachers keep this sacred tradition alive. For a few minutes each week, we build hermeneutical bridges. Standing before God and the church, we lead people in spiritual discernment, showing the congregation how to read the voices of Scripture and discern how those words can come back through our bodies.

In that time, whether there are ten people or two thousand in our congregation, we pastors try to make it over the hermeneutical bridge and say something about the difficulties that young adults face. We try to speak to what they're feeling and realize that the context of many people under forty might be different from the rest of the congregation. That does not mean that we need to roll out the PowerPoint presentations, latest pop cultural references, or mediocre rock music. Instead, we do what churches are really good at doing: we care and we preach. When we understand the context of young adults and listen to them, without smugly dismissing or denying their realities, we begin to connect with those under forty in our midst, where they live and how they live.

When preaching to people in their twenties and thirties, when we make it to the other side of the hermeneutical bridge, we speak to their loneliness and isolation. We can talk about the work stress and the mommy wars. We can communicate the grief surrounding infertility and miscarriages. Our churches articulate the heartache of war, the guilt of torture, and the fear of terrorism. We can verbalize the remorse of parenting and the anxiety of taking care of our own parents.

In our churches, we offer hope in times of desperate need. While pointing out the feelings of alienation in our nomadic lives, we speak of the body of Christ, in which each person has a function and becomes a part of a supportive environment. While opening up the fear of failure that young adults try hard to swallow back, we tell of a loving God whose outstretched arms welcome the prodigal home. While the world seems to explode in complicated wars, we speak Jesus's simple command to love our neighbors as we love ourselves.

As we understand the depression and anxiety that our children live with as our most vulnerable audience in a highly commercialized culture, we speak of an abundant life through Jesus Christ. When we realize the damage that our petroleum dependence causes to our environment, we speak of stewardship, caring for God's creation, and the responsible ways that we can nurture our resources. Each Sunday, we have an opportunity to take people across that hermeneutical bridge and talk about something that matters.

Prayer

Spiritual communities also form with prayer. That strange meandering path on which God meets us looks different for each person, and
finding it takes time. That's a major investment that people usually
don't have, but for some reason, God rarely shows us what to do with
neon signs and flashing lights as we speed along the highway. God
meets us in the intentional hours of prayer.

CONTEMPLATIVE PRAYER

When I asked pastors in their twenties and thirties what sort of practices they lead young adults in, almost every one of them spoke about
the practice of contemplative prayer, or sitting in silent meditation.
David Gambrell, a minister who has been engaged in teaching congregations about contemplative worship for several years, reflected,
"I've found young adults—from high school students to thirty-somethings—to be quite receptive to and appreciative of this approach to
liturgy. Many of us are weary of words, thirsty for silence, hungry
for symbols that nourish the imagination."

I certainly experienced this hunger when Vivien Kilner, a
spiritual director, artfully led a contemplative prayer group in our
congregation, moving us gently from silence to discussion. In one
of the moments of reflection, Lauren Lien, a twenty-four-year-old
musician, writer, and church leader, compared sitting in the prayerful
stillness with sitting in an orchestra: "There is that short time, right
after the instruments tune up, and everyone is leaning in, waiting
for the conductor. The whole concert hall is filled with silence. It's an
amazing moment when people anticipate the symphony, in silence,
knowing that the next few moments will never happen again in quite
that same way."

I leaned in and understood. We constantly fill our lives with
things: the morning radio hosts bickering, the angry political pundits,
the reviews of every movie. We watch the Weather Channel, following the green bit-mapped graphics of every cloud formation, until
we forget to look into the sky and listen to our aching knee to predict
the storm. We don't form our opinions on the news until we hear the

talking points of others. We do not watch a movie until we've read the reviews. We are separated from our own feelings and opinions as we take on the voice of another, and we forget how to pray.

To sit in quiet, we are beckoned to hear our own unencumbered expressions and listen for God's Spirit stirring. In this important practice, we quiet the proliferation of words, lower them into our hearts, and let them rest. It can be difficult, because it is not always joy that we experience; it is also our sadness, grief, and heartache. We have the immediate urge to turn on the TV, check the e-mail, do the dishes, or do anything to get us out of our own thoughts.

We will wish that our fathers had told us that they were proud of us, or that our mothers could have been happy. We will fear financial failure and our hearts will sing the sad song of loneliness. Our grief will wash over us, as we suddenly remember how much we loved the smooth skin of our grandmother, or we wonder why we could not keep our college friend from taking his life. We will cry for the miscarried child, and for the children that we will never have.

Things surface from ten years ago, and we might begin to wonder, "Why am I thinking about that? Surely I should be over that by now. There must be something really wrong with me." But there's not. We just never fully felt the passion surrounding that situation, or we never gave ourselves enough space to grieve. Instead we've been carrying it around in our tense shoulders or our aching stomachs. Our own emotions may frighten us, as we feel like our broken selves will never be put back together again. Sitting completely still, in silence, we may feel like we are out of control.

In the calm, we learn to listen to ourselves and for God. We tune into that still small voice and enfold our hurts as we would surround our own weeping child. With patient care, we place her gently on our lap, rock her back and forth, and smooth out her tangled hair. Looking into the wound, we clean it out, even though it stings, and then we smell all the rich tones of her scalp, loving her deeply.

As we do, gradually, we realize the arms of God growing up around us, and our lonely, searching desperation can rest with a parent who loves us deeply, who pats our back, untangles our hair, and adores the smell of our scalp. In silence, we learn to rest, embraced by God, whose arms ache with love for us, who longs to spend a moment with us, who has been looking for a quiet chance to whisper, "You are my beloved child. I am well pleased with you."

When our contemplative prayer group ended, the members decided to keep meeting periodically, because they not only had a renewed sense of the presence of God, but the relationships between the members had grown deep.

It was strange. Because we did not spend much time talking, I did not expect that sense of community to form. But then I remembered a couple of years after my husband and I began dating, when our moments became stilled of the nervous, endless chatter, and we could share comfortable silence together. I knew then that our relationship had grown deeper. Now, years later, we cherish each morning together, waking up before our child, sipping coffee, reading, writing, and listening only to the song of the birds. The peace feeds our relationship.

It must have happened that way in that group. The silence allowed for a deep connection.

Walking Meditation

It was in a time of turmoil when I began the practice of walking meditation and realized the importance of embodied prayers. The aging congregation in Rhode Island that I pastored had a steady stream of dying members. Each time I buried someone, I soon got another call about a dear friend in intensive care, or a kind man who had just passed quickly and quietly. Intense waves of grief washed over the family members, and as I sat with the loved ones, I longed to have someone sit with me.

In the midst of this, I had an early miscarriage. I felt life and hope drain out of me, but I still didn't have the support that pastors need in their own periods of sadness, denial, and bargaining. I said goodbye to a couple of close friends who moved away, and could not find much strength to fill the void. In my empty pain, the congregational criticism that often comes with being a pastor wounded me deeply.

It was a dark year in my life, and I stumbled and tripped all the way through it. I didn't know how to ask for help, and when I did, I had the terrible feeling that somehow needing it was the wrong thing. I figured that other pastors must have gone through the same things, but talking to others in the denomination about my weaknesses made me feel . . . well, weak. My well-meaning colleagues would tell me that I needed to toughen up and develop thicker skin. But I didn't know how to love a flock like a shepherd and not allow the loss to bother me.

In the darkening days of one New England fall, I put on several layers of clothing, prepared a thermal mug of tea, and walked along the bike path next to my home. A quarter of a mile south, I saw a passageway cut through the marsh. I ducked through the brown cattails and wandered on a thin path worn only by a few summertime fishermen. At times, I could barely follow the muddy meandering trail, until it finally led to a wide, desolate, sandy beach, where I began to meet God.

The rocks first whispered that I stood on holy ground. I leapt from boulder to boulder over a small stream to get to the sandy shore, and on the way, I heard the gentle rolling of water. Balancing on the dry spots of the jutting boulders, I searched for a place to sit. Hugging my knees to my chest, I spent the next moments staring at the smooth brown, green and gray stones. Studying the rich texture and layers of each hard surface, I found that it was just like Jesus said on Palm Sunday: when I was quiet, even the rocks cried out in praise.

My breath deepened and the flowing water seemed to reach into me until I found tears streaming down my face. I began to wipe them off and choke them back, until I looked around the shore. I was alone. In that place, I didn't have to be a nonanxious presence for anyone else and my tears didn't need an accompanying apology. My skin could be as thin as paper, and I could finally feel the hollow, aching loss.

After a long while, I reached the end of my own stream, stood up, stretched my stiff legs and began to follow the shoreline. Walking along the beach put me in touch with another rhythm. My body no longer raced with the piercing ring of the phone or the beat of the copy machine. My eyes did not squint from the computer screen's glare, and I was not busy scribbling something into my full calendar. I wasn't driving at 55 miles per hour. I wasn't talking, or preaching, or making something happen. I was just there, hearing the pattern of my own breath for the first time in a long while. Breathing steadily and gently, I noticed that the pulse of my steps slowed to the beat of the pounding shore, and the blood moved through my veins in the same cadence. It was a slower tempo than I was used to, one that I had forgotten.

My body began to resonate with the patterned measures of the few singing birds. The crickets whistled out a tempo like a distant crazed gym teacher and the chilly wind blew on my back, until I sensed the ancient breath of God moving me and soothing me.

Understanding Paul Tillich's divine metaphor in a new way, the Ground of Being pulsed beneath me, the trees of the field clapped their hands, and the water's brilliance reflected God's radiance. And I found that the depth of my sorrow was matched with an abundant peace.

After that first walk, I began to steal away-time; like the young Beloved in the Song of Songs, I would secretly fit an hour into my day to walk and pray. It was an extravagance that I had never allowed myself before in my work week, with my strong belief that a part of a pastor's ministry of presence comes with a healthy amount of time in the office, but I desperately craved the solitude.

I began to realize that if I was going to be a helpful pastoral presence at the deathbed, I had to carve out the time to replenish myself. Ignoring my imagined critics whispering in my empty office, I realized that I could not lead my congregation on a path to meet God unless I found one myself.

As the white oyster shells crunched beneath my tennis shoes, I realized that support came from the earth below me, that the air that I breathed sustained me, and that the beauty of the turning leaves nourished me. Slowly, I was healed by all that surrounded me as I realized that in God I lived and moved and had my being. Through the beauty of creation, I began to rest in the certain knowledge that God loved me.

Even in that time of professional isolation, I began to feel a part of something larger than myself. When I saw a cold and wounded baby bird, I sensed my own fragility. When I discovered some ancient stone walls mysteriously lining the beach, I found a new strength within me. When I glimpsed a tiny jellyfish, dancing close to the shore like a miniature pink tutu that had lost its ballerina, I laughed with excitement. As I explored the shells scattered about the coast, noticing the distinct color, texture, and beauty of each one, I began to sense the abundance of our great God.

Writing sermons, I prayed for direction and began to dig deeper, unearthing emotions that I had tried to keep tightly packed down. Each Saturday morning, I spent preparation time with my nose in books and with my nose following the scent of drying seaweed, until the words flowed.

In the year to come, I looked forward to those times, when I could be alone on the secret beach. I watched as the orange and yellow leaves could no longer cling to the trees, until the branches turned black and naked against the skyline. The rocks became ice-covered and slippery, and the limbs filled with snow. After many months of dark winter, the tips of the spring blooms began to peek out of the ground and I found starfish lining the shore. Then, everything came into full bloom at the height of that New England summer.

As I walked, I prayed and listened, hearing my own hopes, thoughts, and dreams. I had space to feel my sorrow, anger, and loss. My sense of enrichment grew alongside the natural variety and richness that surrounded me. A renewed sense of responsibility to care for God's creation ignited within me. With each careful and slow step, I realized that even though my path was one giant circle, I was being led.

Through these embodied prayers, as I became attached to creation and to the Creator, I began to understand the importance of incarnational practices that connect us with God and one another. The importance of solitude and community became clearer. As Parker Palmer wrote, "we need solitude and community simultaneously. . . . Together, they make us whole, like breathing in and breathing out."[2]

In these flat-screened days when we fill our hours with disembodied cell phone voices, we will need to look for ways in which we can develop spiritual communities by being physically present with each other, engaging our senses, drawing out stories, preaching relevant sermons, and connecting with God.

Reflection Questions

1. How does modern technology affect communities? Share a story of connection or loss that has come with different forms of communication.

2. In your church, what sort of support do the members give to your pastor so that he or she can cultivate the art of preaching? Does your congregation understand the importance of allowing the pastor time away from the office to prepare sermons? Do the members allow for continuing education?

3. Does your church have a time in which members can tell stories about their lives? If not, what might that opportunity look like in your congregation?

4. What disciplines do the leadership of your church practice? How do the traditions in your church engage the senses?

5. How could you form spiritual communities in your congregation? What would a spiritual community look like in your neighborhood and demographic context?

CHAPTER 8

Growing Life

When I was starting out as a twenty-seven-year-old pastor, all I could think of was how much our congregation needed to grow, change, revitalize, and transform. Then I attended a small church seminar, thinking that this would teach me how to do all of those things. It gave me a much greater gift.

The facilitator began with the words: "You are enough." Then she repeated them, "You are enough." She spoke to my church, that handful of elderly people who were so afraid of death. She spoke to me, a young short pastor who looked like she had barely graduated from high school. She spoke to my perfectionism and my drive to succeed, and she spoke to my deep longing and desire to reach out to young adults. And she was right. The mainline denominational church has everything that it needs to minister to younger generations.

When they think about developing spiritual community for young adults, most people tend to envisage a megachurch, with arena seats and surround sound. This model makes reaching out to people in their twenties and thirties seem impossible for the small denominational church. The rock-concert church settings appeal to many people in their forties and fifties, and their rise has become a well-tracked cultural and religious phenomenon since the 1980s to 1990s. They are often iconoclastic in style and conservative in theology. This way of being church certainly has a place in our society. Indeed, I grew up in a megachurch. Unfortunately, for me, it was a place where I rarely celebrated the sacraments and was regularly scandalized by the sexual misconduct of our pastoral leadership.

When I chose my congregation as an adult, I did not want a charismatic rock star as a pastor. I hoped for a minister who knew my name. I craved to be in a place where people noticed if I was missing on a Sunday morning. I looked for a church where I could serve God and connect with members surrounding me. I wished for a congregation who cared for the poor, hungry, and disadvantaged in our streets and around the world. I wanted to be in a church that protected the environment. I needed to be a part of a history and a rich tradition. I desired a church that challenged and proclaimed the progressive theology that grew up inside of me. And I yearned to be in a congregation where the young and old gathered, together.

My worship pattern mirrored where many of my friends were going. I watched as they went through the changes of young adulthood: many of them married, others came out of the closet, some had children, a few divorced, and all experienced the tragedy of death. Most of my friends no longer attend church, but those who do traveled from Christian Missionary Alliance to Episcopal, from Pentecostal to Lutheran, from Baptist to Presbyterian, or from Assembly of God to Methodist. Each person chose small and medium-sized churches with wonderful tradition and liturgy.

Our experiences are common, as Diana Butler Bass points out in *The Practicing Congregation: Imagining a New Old Church.* She tracks the young adult's move away from Baby Boomer-led megachurches to "small to medium-sized congregations with more liturgical forms of worship."[1]

It makes sense. Young adults do not need an entertaining experience that happens to them; rather, they need connection, a place where they can be grounded in a spiritual community.

Intergenerational Connection

We are now feeling the aftermath of the evangelical boom of the seventies, eighties, and nineties. The back door, it appears, may have been as wide open as the front door, for the adults who grew up in those folding pew chairs or arena seats are now wandering, looking for a spiritual home, and it is the mainline church that now has the gifts that many twenty- and thirty-year-olds crave. This will be a ripe and rich season for our church—if our congregations can learn to receive these young adults.

If church leadership imagines that introducing an electronic keyboard and twenty minutes of praise choruses is enough to attract people in their twenties and thirties, then they might want to rethink their evangelistic efforts. Right now, there is a widespread generational rejection of contemporary worship that has to do with a young adult's resistance to becoming a market sample or part of a target audience.

On the shadow side of growing megachurches and mega-styled-churches has been a rising disgust for these highly commercialized religious products. John Austin, who worked as an artist in the Christian music industry where most praise choruses originate, once bravely noted to a top executive, "It seems like the Contemporary Christian Music is like a commercial venture with a thin coating of spirituality."

"No," the executive corrected him, "It's all commercial."

Many adults spent their younger years targeted by this particular segment of the church, and they're uncomfortable with the consequences. When a church treats its members like consumers, at the end of the day, they feel like consumers. That's a very prickly sensation for people in their twenties and thirties, especially when they have been the chief losers in this market economy.

Instead of Boomer-style worship that caters to one particular age group, churches can entwine an intergenerational community that connects with God, each other, and the world. Pastors, elders, and deacons will work nimbly, like carpet weavers, putting the intricate and various colored threads of tradition and community together, making sure that there is space for young adults and that the connections are tight. They will begin by understanding the context of young adults and responding to them in meaningful ways.

Economic Consideration

Before we can minister to the missing generation, we need to recognize their context. One major force that drives people in their twenties and thirties is their economic situation, particularly their tremendous debt load. It causes sons to move back to their parents' homes in their twenties, it forces dating couples to transfer away from each other and put off committed relationships. It makes the strain on families with children unbearable. Now, even with two people in every household working at least one job, they have less spending money than their parents did in the seventies.[2] Bankruptcies boom, as people can no longer live under their staggering debt.

Yet young adults don't talk about their economic situations, even if their credit card bill keeps them awake every night. Ours is a culture in which honesty about our finances can never be discussed, especially if one is struggling. In fact, churches drive young adults away by their perpetuation of the notion that financial blessing is a thumbs up from God and economic failure signals a moral problem in a person.

The economic situation affects everything in a young adult's life, and it has a huge impact on their ability to form committed relationships. Many people in their twenties and thirties often find that they cannot bind themselves to loving relationships, civic institutions, or spiritual communities because they cannot make the commitments of finances, time, or trust.

The inability to trust is crucial. In their economic landscape, young adults pay for the nation's tax cuts through their student loans. In their employment, they pay for corporate profits by taking temporary jobs without insurance, benefits, or a livable wage. In real estate, they learn to become permanent renters, sending their monthly check to a landlord.

In all of these situations, our society has not taken care of young adults. We do not support their education, bodies, children, or future. Their ample opportunities for debt have raised the standard of living, but left them with a hidden scarcity. Meanwhile, we berate twenty- and thirty-year-olds for their economic and moral failures if they do not become completely self-sufficient at eighteen. We write them off as too entitled or selfish and don't take into account the larger picture in which they live.

What would happen if churches begin to talk about these issues? Modeling the prophets, we often discuss the injustices in our society. What if we took the same care with our young adults? Are there ways in which we as congregations engage in conversations that heap criticism on young adults and equate economic instability with moral failure? Could we have the courage to end our practice of checking the resumes of our visitors and showing subtle intolerance for middle and lower classes? If we begin to act with some economic understanding, we might begin building trust with these wounded generations. Slowly and carefully, we can take steps toward healing the breach.

In response to financial instabilities, we can begin to focus on what Jesus means when he said, "I come that you might have life and have it abundantly." It sounds strange to hear this promise of abundance for a commercial-weary, debt-ridden, stressed-out generation. But in our congregations, we're called to look for ways to create an environment where abundance is found in spiritual and incarnational community.

Unambiguous Inclusion

As we start to understand the context of young adults, we begin making room for them, allowing them to have their points of view, even on controversial topics.

The front page of the *Washington Post* said it: "Faiths Condemn Homosexuality."[3] In the article, the Roman Catholic Church, Baptist Church, and Presbyterian Church were named as inhospitable places for gay and lesbians. I saw the headline and I knew it was going to be a frustrating day at the office.

"I am so embarrassed," Erica Swanson, a young member and the convener of our deacons at Western, complained on the phone. "It makes us look homophobic. Everyone knows I'm Presbyterian. They're going to think that's what I believe, but our church isn't like that at all!" I got e-mails too, from other young members wondering if we could do something about what was happening.

There was nothing we could do. Our stance on LGBT ordination in the Presbyterian Church (USA) is complicated and nuanced. There was no way to sum it up in a pithy letter to the editor. It's ambiguous, vague, and confusing.

This complex position has been important in keeping a tenuous unity in our church, but it is not good for reaching out to young adults. Most people in their twenties and thirties have loved ones who are

openly gay or lesbian and they don't want to be associated with organizations and institutions that discriminate against people with
differing orientations. If they read on the cover of the newspaper
that a denomination condemns homosexual leadership, most people
under forty will feel alienated from that church.

Young adults see great value in diversity, including different
sexual orientations, ethnicities, and religious backgrounds. In our
congregations, we do well to understand how much we offend and
drive away young adults when we lift up exclusive views on sexuality
and soteriology.

Young adults often feel conflicted when they attend churches
that condemn homosexuality and the beliefs of their family and
friends. They become embarrassed about inviting their neighbors
to church, because they are afraid that their friends will be offended
in the service. If we want to minister to people in their twenties and
thirties, we do well to back off from the bickering that excludes so
many younger members, and we can begin welcoming and affirming
the differences in our society.

I look at my tribe, my small group of friends with whom I keep in
constant contact. A couple of them are pastors, but most are largely
unlike me. They are gay, straight, single, and married. Some have
children, but most do not. They are Buddhist, agnostic, and Christians. They are all loving, caring, and responsible people with whom I
have grown for many years. Some barely scrape by while others make
a lot of money. We crisscross the continent, and have changed many
of our political, philosophical, and theological beliefs.

I am often surprised that they consider me a part of their made-
up family, especially with my career choice. But they do. They have
been tolerant of me for many years and I'm often overwhelmed by
their kindness and support.

As I have gotten older, I can't imagine worshiping in a place that
couldn't accept my tribe. I love them. And I know that God is much
more gracious than I could ever be, so God must love them too. I long
for a spiritual community that reflects that love, a body that could
welcome and affirm all of us.

People in their twenties and thirties generally have much more
progressive views on religion, politics, and sexuality. For many of them,

going to a church where their opinions are regularly disregarded is like attending an uncomfortable holiday reunion where their family's constantly watching Fox News and they're trying not to talk about all the war protests in which they've participated in the last year.

Most young adults believe in tolerance and inclusion in the very core of their being, and no one is going to convert them, change them, or convince them otherwise. But they can find places to rest, to form tribes, if mainline congregations begin to make room for them. When congregations allow for the convictions of young adults, for their deep desire to love their neighbor as they love themselves, then we can begin practicing affirming traditions.

Affirming Traditions

I sat down at a card table with my husband and a stranger. The table was on the stage of a fellowship hall, and the giant room was filled with old books, records, dishes and clothes. I looked down at my plate, piled high with sausage. The smell of sauerkraut and mildewing pages filled the air. As I surveyed the workers tending the food and rummage sale, I could see they were all well over seventy. The cashier had a handwritten poster above her head announcing that she was in her nineties.

After a little small talk, I became acquainted with the woman next to me. "They're not going to be able to have this German lunch much longer, you know."

I shook my head, noting, "Yes. I can imagine that it takes a lot of work to pull this off."

"My friends put this together. They work on it for nine months out of the year. They've been having this sale for decades. And now, the younger members in the congregation, they want nothing to do with it!"

I swallowed hard and shook my head some more. "Yes. Well, it is held at noon on a Thursday. Most women work now, so this is a very difficult time for them to be running a fundraiser."

She stabbed her sausage with a fork as she continued, "Oh, they've been preparing for this in the evenings—and on weekends. The young women in the church just won't do it. They just don't have that same sense of commitment."

I listened as she continued to explain exactly how many years the lunch had been served, how all the money went to missions, how it would be a terrible shame for the entire neighborhood if this could not continue. Her grief and anger about the sale was as bitter as the sauerkraut.

She couldn't understand my attempts to explain that it takes most households at least two salaries to live in D.C. and that leaves very little time for people to take on fundraising projects that last for over nine months. She simply determined that young mothers today just don't have the necessary motivation and sacrifice to make these things work. And so she parted, with a civil smile and a clearly irritated, "Goodbye."

We have growing tensions in our congregations. We have the sausage dinner on one end of the table and young adults on the other. Churches clearly need to be on the side of the young adults, but for some reason, they often take the side of the sausage dinner instead.

Some of the customs of our churches no longer make sense in the hectic schedules of young adults. Can we rethink committees that take two hours to table every issue for six months and fundraising sales that have alarming labor-to-production ratios? Can we imagine how to run our churches with fewer volunteer hours by making our meetings more efficient and perhaps by giving more decision-making power to our ministers?

Many of our congregations rely on committee work to build community, but younger generations often yearn for something else when they gather together. This alienated group wants to connect in meaningful ways.

Our meetings should certainly reflect the church's larger purpose to serve our Creator, to live as Jesus Christ, and to be empowered by the Holy Spirit. Yet, our spiritual traditions should not solely take place within the deliberate point-by-point agenda items of committee meetings. Younger generations need affirming traditions that

1. take into account their time and schedules,
2. provide for the entire family,
3. enhance connections with God, each other, and the world.

Account for Time and Schedules

First, if there is reluctance for the next generation to take over some of the customs of our congregations, we need to grieve that loss, but we have to let some things go. People in their twenties and thirties just may not have the time in their schedules to put into the difficult and meaningful customs that have built up over the years.

Can we churches resist the temptation to heap criticism on young adults for their lack of commitment to the church? Instead, can we begin listening for traditions that mean something to them? Can we stop expecting them to abide by an invisible rulebook, and allow them the space and opportunity to nurture their own spiritual traditions in our congregations?

Provide for the Entire Family, Singles, and Extended Families

Second, we need to think about families as units. "People act as if we don't have a child," one thirty-seven-year-old dad shook his head as he explained the frustration of trying to participate in a planning committee in the United Church of Christ. "We spent days trying to get childcare for our son so that we could participate in this meeting, and after it was all set, we got an e-mail the night before saying that they changed the date! The committee's filled with retired people. They didn't care if there was a last-minute change, but there was no consideration for us as parents, or for our child."

If we want to encourage parents to be involved in planning and events, we can begin to provide childcare. Parents often use up their babysitting resources so that they can work. They juggle their schedules and their children in thoughtful ways, hoping to provide the best that they can for their sons and daughters. After being away from their children all day, they usually want to be with them at the end of the evening. So, if we invite a dad or mom to participate, let's realize how that affects children and understand that there probably will not be another parent at home to take care of the kids.

Likewise, we can understand the needs of caretakers, who tend to elderly parents. We can extend our consideration to people who have the responsibility for mentally ill, mentally challenged, or disabled adults.

If we begin to realize of the interconnectedness of individuals, we can open our churches to the presence and gifts of many more people.

If we want children in our services, we need to take the basic steps to welcome them, by painting our nurseries, child-proofing our churches, and making sure that there is adequate care and meaningful things for them to do. Even if there are no children in the church, congregations need to start with these steps because these visible signs of hospitality will go a long way when a family with young children shows up on a Sunday morning.

Enhance Connections with God, Each Other, and the World

Third, we must realize that affirming traditions will connect our congregations to God, each other, and the world. In a time of increased alienation, young adults come to church to practice spiritual traditions, meet friends, and participate in social justice. Our churches are the perfect places and communities in which to provide the space for these things to happen. We do well to present opportunities for people to enrich their spiritual lives. We can make a space for young adults to meet and care for one another in social settings, outside of committee meetings.

We know a great deal about what is happening in the world and on our streets, and it can make us feel hopeless. As we pass by homeless people, we want them to have food and warmth. When we witness the atrocities of war and genocide, we need to have a sense that our spiritual communities are doing something to speak out, that they are places of hope, and that participating in them can make a difference.

As we begin affirming traditions in our churches allowing welcome participation from young adults, then we can share our leadership with them.

Sharing Leadership

A member of Western Presbyterian, who is preparing to attend seminary, confesses to me, "I'm sorry. But I google. I'm in my twenties, and that's just what we do."

"What?" I laugh in confusion, wondering why she feels the need to confess that she uses an Internet search engine.

"If I'm interested in a committee, a board, or an organization, I google each and every member on it."

Laughing harder, I understand, because I do the same thing. It's a litmus test, of sorts. I often determine the efficacy of a denomination, church, or organization by looking to see who's on their board. I'm not searching for a long list of resume credentials; rather, I observe to see if the organization's decision-making body is made up of only one particular age, gender, and ethnic demographic, or if it includes people of color, women, or anyone under forty-five.

If diversity is not represented, then I know they'll have great difficulty maintaining viability in the years to come. It's not a matter of reverse discrimination. In contrast, our population pool has become so diverse that if the majority of the leadership in a particular organization looks alike, then their nominating committees have left out a significant portion of people. Their pool of prospective members has become too small; they're fishing out of a bedroom aquarium instead of the Atlantic Ocean. Therefore, they cannot be choosing the most insightful and innovative leadership.

The most crucial aspect when developing intergenerational ministry is making sure that people under the age of forty-five hold leadership positions. As we begin to trust younger people in our congregations and governing bodies, as we allow them to have some power, then our churches will reflect that leadership.

Developing leadership needs to occur long before our nominating committees meet. As our denominational headship grows whiter, we can spend less energy holding on to our positions and put more effort in mentoring others. As we start actively identifying young adults in our midst and spending time with them, we can find ways to encourage and support them. As we seek out the talents and abilities of young adults, we can listen to their opinions and mentor them in all of our leadership positions.

This doesn't mean assembling a focus group of young adults and having a group of sixty-year-olds implement the fresh ideas into their established vision of the organization. This doesn't mean giving a twenty-year-old a few hundred dollars to develop an intriguing Web site. Although these might be important beginning steps, significant ministry to a new generation will occur when we listen to the voices of young adults regularly, when their insight becomes crucial in forming our vision, when we encourage people in their twenties and thirties to have some space around the table every month.

In all levels, young adults seem to be absent in our mainline denominations. I often sit in nominating committees, hearing the conversations of people who do not necessarily want to choose the same old people year after year, but they don't feel as if they have any other choice. They can only see older people surrounding them.

It's much easier to schedule meetings with retired people. They want to fill leadership positions with their friends; after all, it's painless to ask someone you know for a favor. The board looks better when it's made up of people with a stream of resume credentials, and people need a lifetime to develop that CV. They want members with financial heft to become aware of the needs of our organizations.

These are all good reasons to choose older members. However, if these exclusive nominating practices continue, they might lead us into a parochial vision of who we are and who we can be. While looking for leaders, we can also save some seats for the great insight and vision that young members provide. Although younger generations do not always have the time for extensive committee meetings, we can find ways to include them in our church governments and leadership.

We will need to share power, not just for the sake of institutional viability, but for the sake of young adults. We can show the next generation what it means to be a part of a caring supportive environment, so they might function as valued members of the body of Christ. We can begin looking for ways to retain our ministers and support young clergy, especially by providing adequate salaries, allowing them to have some influence, refraining from unconstructive and unnecessary criticism, and hiring more women as senior ministers and heads of staff.

As we begin to trust younger people in our congregations, pulpits, and governing bodies, and we allow them to have some power, then our churches will reflect that leadership.

Spiritual Guidance

Finally, we minister to the missing generation with spiritual guidance. We can respond to the alienation and isolation of younger generations with incarnational ministries, which care for our spirits and bodies. By creating supportive environments where physical presence is valued, honesty is allowed, and difficulties are named, our spiritual lives will deepen. We can open ourselves to a healing process, so that people can be grounded in their communities and their land. We can nurture healthy attachments and create a culture of abundance.

Nurture Healthy Attachment

Peter Fischer, a Lutheran minister in Vancouver, British Columbia, presides over an incarnational ministry when he blesses the bicycles in his city. Each year, cyclists gather on the church steps, and Pete leads a liturgy that affirms their relationship to the Creator and the creation. He upholds their choice to care for their bodies and environment with sustainable transportation. He guides the cyclists, bus riders, and walkers in a time of remembrance for those who have died while riding in the streets. He anoints the chains with 3-in-1 oil and the cyclists with sunscreen. In the process, he supports the important choices of young adults in prayers that make those who gather a bit more grounded.

Encourage Abundance

In our high consumer, higher debt society, we have created an external bounty that hides our internal scarcity. We have more, but we end up with less. In contrast, in our spiritual communities, silence speaks louder than shouting, giving fills us more than getting, and less is often more. To encourage a culture of abundance in our churches, we need to reclaim our time, rethink our programming, and reconsider our space.

To begin reclaiming our time, we can relearn how to keep the Sabbath, how to give people a chance to rest. In our church, John Wimberly began noticing a trend of people who kept heavy work schedules all week and then, instead of enjoying their Sabbath, would pack up their cars with heavy bags and drive for hours on weekend "escapes" or "breaks." Visiting friends, going to weddings, celebrating birthdays—they were doing wonderful things, but the problem was that they never allowed their foot off the pedal or gave themselves a chance to rest. John began talking about it and writing newsletter articles that resonated with the congregation. And it seemed that many of them heeded the advice and slow down.

Just as exhausted soil needs fallow time to replenish itself, our bodies long for rest. We crave a sacred time, time set aside, time in which we do not buy or sell, we do not accumulate or produce, but we learn to restore ourselves. Our congregations are the perfect places for people to go when they are weary and heavy-laden. As church, we already have a long tradition of fasting and savoring a Sabbath, even if it's one we need to rediscover.

Within the stress of the workweek, with our packed calendars, we can learn to rest. It does not have to be on a Saturday or a Sunday, but we can take a day and set it aside to renew our souls. Even when our e-mail inboxes are full of exciting last-minute, one-night getaway packages, we can turn off the computer and recover our strength. Even with the endless demands of our jobs, we can ignore the cell phones and pagers for a day. Even with the pull to entertain our children, we can stay home from the mall. When we embrace God's good gift of renewal, we can gain perspective on our lives.

While we're at it, perhaps we can also reconsider our programming for families. As the pastor of small to medium congregations, I often hear, "I love this church. I really do. But there's just not enough here for my child." While many people in their twenties and thirties prefer small churches, there is a sense that when a child is born, these parents feel the need to find something else for their children.

When speaking to these concerned moms and dads, I point out the Sunday school, Christmas pageant, Easter play, and fall family party. But that's not enough. I talk about how I know all of the children by name, and that I work hard to build a relationship with each child so that they can have a spiritual guide. But that's not enough. I explain how much their child means to the older members of the congregation. But that's not enough. The church was wonderful for the parents, but they just want more for their children: more programs, more socialization with other children, and more opportunities for them.

I understand. But it also makes me sad. As a mom myself, I have a vision that church will become a place for families to rest. We are weary of the consumer culture that has hit our children full-force and left us feeling inadequate on every front. We know that our kids ought to be playing at least five sports per year and working hard to get those scholarships to the most prestigious schools. We know that birthdays should be highly planned, themed, and orchestrated events with at least three activity tables to keep our child's attention active at every moment. We recognize the overwhelming expectations for children to be entertained and challenged at a high level at all times.

Yet maybe our churches can be notable precisely by being different. In a small congregation, we may not be able to coordinate events at the level of a well-organized, program-oriented church, but we can provide many of the things that our highly scheduled lives might need: intergenerational relationships, the care of a community, and even a chance for our child to be a little bored (a highly underrated opportunity in our society). Many small congregations do not have the level of participation for a lot of programming, but most of them can provide a loving, supportive environment for them while they grow up.

Children need that place right now. They have learned to be consumers, they are experts on being entertained, but they need an opportunity to rest in a simple caring community as much as any of us.

Associate pastors in large congregations often say they felt more like cruise directors than ministers. Their shepherding has become more about managing a herd of people to get from one program to the next. They look exhausted from running a bevy of events, keeping up with their full calendars, and attending every evening and weekend meeting. If they are tired, and running the programs is their job, imagine how their congregants must feel.

Finally, as we consider creating a spiritual community of abundance, we may need to rethink our worship spaces. Corey Sanderson, the thirty-seven-year-old founding pastor of the Potter's House in

Traverse City, Michigan, appreciates the abundance that the Potter's House has because they have no building. "We can do ministry instead of maintenance," he says happily. He knows the mire that congregations can get into when keeping up with the leaky roof, the rusty pipes, and the impossible boiler becomes the sole mission of the church. "When churches spend all of their money, time, and energy on a building that crumbles around them, they're just in a constant losing battle. Churches should start selling their buildings."

Of course, selling the building is not a good option for most churches, but it works for the Potter's House. Corey has great flexibility because his church congregates in a Quaker meeting house and they can easily move outside for special services and picnics. They are not weighed down by the expense of a building. But there's more than that: because the church's mission, worship, and identity are not tied to bricks and mortar, it is more bound to God and the community.

In the years to come, our mammoth worshiping spaces may become more and more difficult to maintain, and we'll need to weigh many factors as we consider our buildings. They can cause a great deal of environmental damage with their energy inefficiency. They also make important contributions to the history, art and architecture of a community. With all of these tensions, we have to consider how much scarcity we create by holding onto our immense edifices.

Our Challenge: Nurturing the Tree of Life

As I think about the urban tribes that surround me in Washington, D.C., I'm reminded of the spiritual practice of a Native American tribe that gives great hope. Its image can become our challenge as we create community in our churches.

The Sioux nation of Nebraska uses a circle in their walking meditation, It's big, a bit like a labyrinth, but this one has only two simple paths intersecting in the middle of it. One runs from west to east, symbolizing our lives, the other from south to north, representing our hardships.

And in the center, where the path of being and adversity meet, a tree of life grows up, strong and beautiful.

I learn of these meditation gardens one hot summer day while visiting the Midwest. The strange thing about Nebraska is that the winter is so harsh that I always expect the summer to be a bit milder, but it's not, and the cruel prairie sun beats down on my head as I take a few moments to walk along the paths. It is wonderful to make it into the center, to see the tree springing up and the birds resting there. The magnificent growth gives shade and beauty. The wind seems to blow more as I stand in the shadow of its limbs, and the tree comforts me, in more ways than one.

It often happens that our spiritual lives can deepen with tragedy. A divorce, a miscarriage, a death, infertility, the loss of a job—these things can shatter us. Living with the pain of abuse, remembering something tightly packed down, or finding out some horrible secret—everyone has walked through suffering. When we don't feel like ourselves and we begin to cry into an exhausted sleep each night, a seed forms within our gut and we are often drawn to the church and to prayer. In times of misfortune, our wounded self cries out for the presence of God.

We begin to ask larger questions and we can almost feel our roots growing deeper as we reach up higher and higher. Our commonplace earth overturns, as we suddenly notice that we need more and a dry thirst begins to evolve. And as we stand in that important place, something swells within us, and like the psalmist proclaims, we become as "trees planted by streams of water, which yield their fruit in its season, and their leaves do not wither."[4]

As we begin to form spiritual communities in our churches, we can recognize that intersection, the place where the lives of young adults meet hardship. If we tend that space with wisdom and care, it is the point where great growth can occur.

At this time, young adults are at a crucial point. Their life paths have crossed with increasing hardship. It's as if younger generations were born on a relational fault line that starting shifting slightly before they came into the world, and continued to rumble under their feet, making everything quiver and roll.

In the United States, women began working more and became less economically dependent on their spouses. Without that dependence, their parents began to renegotiate the basis of marriage and relationships. The positive changes that the Baby Boomers brought to so many areas of life continued as older generations married.

I am extremely grateful to all the men and women who came before me, and allowed me to have a career, a child, and a loving home, but I know that making those initial modifications was not easy. As a result, when the personalities and characters of young adults were forming, the term "dysfunctional family" became a popular and an apt description for most families.

Divorce rates soared in the seventies, to the highest they have ever been in modern times. As these marriages sadly fell apart, the children in the houses were left broken as well. In the years that they were nurtured and formed, they were also going through custody and property battles. As one woman described it, some became, to a greater or lesser extent, victims of "marital carnage."[5]

When children of the 70s and 80s began to attend college, the public funding for post-high school education dropped, and just as it became clear that a person needed a college education to make it into the middle class, it became economically more challenging for them to get a degree. They felt another fissure in the plates; their foundation became shaken, as they learned to rely heavily on student loans and credit cards.

As young adults begin their careers, they still feel the shifting and trembling, as it's more difficult to find steady employment. They are paid by the job, for the hours worked. Without any assurance of employment beyond their next assignment, they have become commodities. They have been stripped of insurance and pensions. They do not have any care for their bodies, their partners, their children, or their future.

As young adults look toward the days set before them, the sight is terrifying. With the careless abuse of the creation, they foresee the possible destruction of many species of animals. They know that there is very little time to change our lifestyle and habits before we lose a great portion of our precious earth.

With the savings accounts of many retirees empty and life expec-
tancy increasing, today's young adults know that nursing their parents
in the next decades will become their responsibility. As our nation
continues to increase our federal deficit, cut taxes for the wealthy,
wage expensive wars, and make endless promises to senior citizens,
young adults realize that the bill will come due soon, and they pray
that their credit cards will not be maxed out when they're left holding
the check.

During this time of abundant national wealth, in our homes,
education, corporations, economy, environment, churches, and government, we have cut costs to the detriment of younger generations. We
have not maintained the foresight to adequately invest in their lives. As a
result, many people in their twenties and thirties do not trust religious,
civic, or political institutions. They are alienated and broken.

Instead of putting hope into communities, younger generations (by
necessity) spend more of their time looking for signs that they will be
fired. They watch for their next job opportunity and scroll the realtor
pages on the Internet so that they can be prepared for their upcoming
move. They expend incredible energy packing and unpacking boxes,
and putting together furniture from Ikea.

Their general context of unrest, resulting from terrorist attacks,
war, instability, and environmental destruction, produces grave personal consequences: a feeling of alienation, a fear of failure, and the
incapacity to form loving relationships.

In this space, a profound thirst grows, as the seed of something
significant searches for the nourishment it needs. There is an increasing feeling of absolute dependence that makes many young adults long
to live with intention and meaning.[6] Meanwhile, they long for caring
bonds in a place in which they can share their loss and abundance,
where their whole selves can be nourished. They yearn for a grounding environment in which they can rest by still waters, where they can
attend to their bodies, souls, and spirits. They long for spiritual communities, where they are formed through preaching, testimony, and
prayer, and where they are fed.

When I talk to people in my generation, they are not only concerned with getting a job with good pay, but also with discerning a

vocation. The hope of kindling new relationships revolves around character compatibility as well as a deeper desire that the choice of a spouse will be the right choice. In the midst of their financial frustrations, unstable employment, and confusing love lives, they want to know that their existence has a deeper purpose. In the face of the destruction that our petroleum dependence and penchant for bombs has created, they long for environments of hope. As our nation neglects to pick up the pieces of the New Orleans levee disaster, they begin to understand the dire inequities that we have created and they ache for a just society. Many people in their twenties and thirties are not only concerned with discerning God's purpose in large decisions, but they become mindful of every step and have a desire to be drawn ever closer to God.

As worshiping communities identify that sacred ground where our lives intersect with adversity, we are called to form nurturing bonds with God, each other, and the world. As we cultivate deeper and richer spiritual lives, we can seek guidance through preaching and prayer. We are well placed to form supportive, tribal communities through listening, talking, and caring, through baptism and communion.

I imagine a wonderful and rich time of growth in the years to come as denominational churches increase in generational understanding. As our congregations begin to share in the right practice of loving our neighbors as we love ourselves, we will grow in tolerance and hospitality. As we develop bonds with God, each other and the world, we will begin to observe the vital traditions that ground us. As we trust and nurture the strengths of our young leaders, our bodies will begin to reflect the rich diversity of young adults. And as we cultivate that ground where our lives intersect with hardship, something miraculous will occur. God will allow that seed to grow up into a rich, nourishing tree. Our congregations stand at that intersection; we are well placed to provide justice, hope, and community.

Reflection Questions

1. Brainstorm (just list ideas, without judgments or criticisms) at least twenty-five things that your congregation could do to foster

intergenerational relationships, encourage economic understanding, cultivate unambiguous inclusions, discover affirming
traditions, promote shared leadership, and nurture spiritual community. Look at your list. Are there two things that your church
can begin within the year? Are there things that they could begin
in the next five years?

𝒩otes

INTRODUCTION

1. Caryle Murphy, "Evangelical Author Puts Progressive Spin on Traditional Faith," *Washington Post*, September 17, 2006.
2. Cathy Lynn Grossman, "View of God Can Reveal Your Values and Politics," *USA Today*, September 12, 2006. Grossman reports on a Baylor University survey of religion and reveals that one in three Americans belong to denominations that are considered evangelical, but only 2.2 percent say that it's the single best term to describe themselves. Laurie Goodstein, "Fearing the Loss of Teenagers, Evangelicals Turn Up the Fire," *New York Times*, October 6, 2006.
3. Mike Regele with Mark Schulz. *Death of the Church* (Grand Rapids: Zondervan Publishing House, 1995).
4. Amy Argetsinger and Roxanne Roberts. "They Grow Up So Fast: Hail Gen X," *Washington Post*, November 26, 2006.
5. Juliet B. Schor. *Born to Buy: The Commercialized Child and the New Consumer Culture* (New York: Scribner, 2004), 56.

CHAPTER 1: TRIBAL CHURCH

1. Anya Kamenetz. *Generation Debt: Why Now Is a Terrible Time to be Young* (New York: Riverhead Books, 2006), 97. Kamenetz reports that the median job tenure of workers from twenty-five to thirty-four is just 2.7 years. With the weakening bond between

employers and employees, she writes "twenty-somethings hold jobs for shorter terms, change industries more often, and have more frequent periods of unemployment and underemployment."

2. Ethan Watters, *Urban Tribes: Are Friends the New Family?* (New York: Bloomsbury Publishing, 2003).
3. Anna Bahny, "The Bank of Mom and Dad," *New York Times,* April 20, 2006.
4. Leonard Sweet, *Soul Tsunami: Sink or Swim in New Millennium Culture* (Grand Rapids: Zondervan Publishing House, 1999).

CHAPTER 2: FOSTERING INTERGENERATIONAL RELATIONSHIPS

1. Melissa Block, "Turn 'Repeller' into Adult-Proof Ringtone," *All Things Considered* (NPR), May 26, 2006.
2. Sue Kovach Shuman, "Couterculture Meets Mall Culture for Grace Slick," *Washington Post,* January 13, 2007.
3. Anya Kamanetz, *Generation Debt: Why Now Is a Terrible Time to Be Young* (New York: Riverhead Books, 2006), 148.
4. Judith Warner, *Perfect Madness: Motherhood in the Age of Anxiety* (New York: Riverhead Books, 2005), 215-216.
5. Kamanetz, *Generation Debt,* 184. In 1970, the median age of a person's first marriage was 20.8 for women and 23.2 for men. In 2004, it was 25.8 and 27.4. The marriage rate is also declining.
6. Jackson Carroll, *God's Potters: Pastoral Leadership and the Shaping of Congregations* (Grand Rapids, MI: Wm. B. Eerdmans, 2006), 117. The minister participants were asked to choose two age groups from Older adults, Middle aged adults, Married young adults, Single young adults, Youth 12-18, and Children to age 12.
7. Robert D. Putnam, *Bowling Alone: The Collapse and Revival of American Community* (New York: Simon and Schuster, 2000).
8. Ethan Watters, *Urban Tribes: Are Friends the New Family?* (New York: Bloomsbury), 124.

9. Sam Roberts, *Who We Are Now: The Changing Face of America in the Twenty-first Century* (New York: Times Books, 2004), 38.

10. Juliet B. Schor, *Born to Buy* (New York: Scribner, 2004), 39.

11. Putnam, *Bowling Alone*, 252. Putnam reports on the percentage of adults who attended church weekly in 1997-1998. For 18-29 year olds, it was 25 percent; for 30-44 year olds, it was 32 percent; for 45-59 year olds, it was 37 percent; and for 60+ year olds, it was 47 percent.

12. Ana June, "Confessions of a Heathen," in *Breeder: Real-life Stories from the New Generation of Mothers*, ed. Ariel Gore and Bee Lavender, 238. (Emeryville, CA: Seal Press, 2001).

CHAPTER 3: ENCOURAGING ECONOMIC UNDERSTANDING

1. Elizabeth Warren and Amelia Warren Tyagi. *The Two-Income Trap: Why Middle-Class Mothers and Fathers Are Going Broke* (New York: Basic Books, 2003), 13.

2. George Lakoff, *Whose Freedom?: The Battle Over America's Most Important Idea* (New York: Farrar, Straus and Giroux, 2006), 152. Lakoff notes that this is a particular idea of conservatives, and their notion of individual cause and effect.

3. Mary Pipher, *The Shelter of Each Other: Rebuilding Our Families* (New York: G. P. Putnam's Sons, 1996), 76.

4. The Presbyterian Panel's "Religious and Demographic Profile of Presbyterians, 2005" reports that the median annual family income is $73,200 for members. Seven percent of members and 4 percent of elders have an annual family income of less that $20,000, while many have incomes of $100,000 or more (32 percent of members and 31 percent of elders).

5. Warren and Tyagi address the "Over-consumption Myth," *Two-Income Trap*, 15-54.

6. Debora Vrana, "Middle Class on the Edge?," MSN Money, accessed on October 29, 2006. The cost of education for four-year public colleges (including tuition, fees, and room and board) increased 44 percent from 2001 to 2005.

7. Stephanie McCrummen, "Flush with Success, and Ready to Spend," *Washington Post*, July 6, 2006. The article reports that Americans will spend 22 billion dollars on remodeling their bathrooms in 2006.

8. Mary Ellen Slayter, "It's Harder for Your Generation," *Washington Post*, November 26, 2006.

9. Kamenetz, *Generation Debt*, 158. More specifically, Sam Roberts reports that the net worth for those younger than 35 was $7,240 and $108,885 for those over 65. *Who We Are Now*, 179.

10. Roberts, *Who We Are Now*, 100.

11. Ibid., 169. Roberts writes, "The gap between rich and poor, which has been increasing since the late 1970s, widened, though more slowly, during the 1990s."

12. Kamenetz, *Generation Debt*, 59.

13. Tamara Draut, *Strapped* (New York: Doubleday, 2006).

14. Vrana, "Middle Class on the Edge?"

15. Kamenetz, *Generation Debt*, 127.

16. Juliet B. Schor, *Born To Buy: The Commercialized Child and the New Consumer Culture* (New York: Scribner, 2004), 10.

17. Steven Greenhouse and David Leonhardt, "Real Wages Fail to Match a Rise in Productivity," *New York Times*, August 28, 2006. Worker productivity rose 16.6 percent from 2000 to 2005, yet the median hourly wage dropped 2 percent since 2003 (after factoring inflation). Corporate profits have been higher due to the decline in the labor's share of income.

18. Draut, *Strapped*.

19. Watters, *Urban Tribes*, 25.

20. Roberts, *Who We Are Now*, 35.

21. Ibid., 179. In 2004, a single woman's median net worth was $23,028, while a married couple's median worth was $91,218.

22. Kamenetz, *Generation Debt*, 184.

22. Ibid., 190. The average age of women when they have their first child went from 21 in 1970 to 25 in 2000. Joyce A Martin, M.P.H., et al., "Births: Final Data for 2004," National Vital Statistics Reports, September 29, 2006, 2. The average age of women at first birth in 2004 was 25.2 years.

23. Ibid, 186.

24. Judith Warner, *Perfect Madness: Motherhood in the Age of Anxiety* (New York: Riverhead Books, 2006).

25. Schor, *Born to Buy,* 69-70.

26. Ibid., 141-175.

27. Warren and Tyagi, *Two-Income Trap,* 6.

28. When I use the term "predatory lending" in this chapter, I'm referring to the practices of some banks that charge higher than average interest to low-income customers and encourage high-risk borrowing. For instance, credit card companies routinely set up tables on college campuses, offering incentives for students to sign up at high rates, even though they may not have any income for four years.

29. Kamanetz, *Generation Debt,* 148.

30. Ibid., 13.

31. Ibid., 80. Kamanetz points out that the young are the first to get laid off. In fact, in the fall of 2001, 95 percent of workers who lost their jobs were under 25.

CHAPTER 4: CULTIVATING UNAMBIGUOUS INCLUSION

1. Jackson W. Carroll, *God's Potters: Pastoral Leadership and the Shaping of Congregations* (Grand Rapids, MI: Wm. B. Eerdmans Publishing Co., 2006), 50.

2. Sam Roberts, *Who We Are Now: The Changing Face of American in the Twenty-first Century* (New York: Times Books, 2004), 112.

3. Jean M. Twenge, *Generation Me: Why Today's Young Americans Are More Confident, Assertive, Entitled—and More Miserable Than Ever Before* (New York: Free Press, 2006), 207.

4. Debbie Howlett, "Demographics Rule Attitude on Gay Relationships," *USA Today,* June 26, 2003. Statistics are according to a May 2003 Gallup pole of 1,005 adults. A more recent *New York Times*/CBS News/MTV poll was reported by Adam Nagournew and Megan Thee in the article "Young Americans Are Leaning Left, New Poll Finds," *New York Times,* June 27, 2007.

5. Twenge, *Generation Me,* 207.

6. E.J. Graff, "How the Culture War Was Won" *The American Prospect,* October 21, 2002.

7. This insight came from reading a great deal of Karen Armstrong's work, especially *The Spiral Staircase: My Climb out of Darkness* (New York: Anchor Books, 2005), a memoir in which she explains this shift in emphasis.

CHAPTER 5: DISCOVERING AFFIRMING TRADITIONS

1. Robert D. Putnam, *Bowling Alone: The Collapse and Revival of American Community* (New York: Simon & Schuster Paperbacks, 2000), 75.
2. Diana Butler Bass, *The Practicing Congregation: Imagining a New Old Church* (Herndon, VA: Alban Institute, 2004), 39.
3. Including travel and drop-off time, a $14 wage times 4 hours would equal $56.
4. He was referring to the book cited above, *Bowling Alone* by Robert Putnam. It's a detailed look at the demise of bowling leagues and what that reflects for our broader society.
5. Bass, *Practicing Congregation*, 42. For more stories of vital congregations engaging tradition, see Diana Butler Bass, *Christianity for the Rest of Us: How the Neighborhood Church Is Transforming the Faith* (San Francisco: HarperSanFrancisco, 2006).

CHAPTER 6: PROMOTING SHARED LEADERSHIP

1. Robert D. Putnam, *Bowling Alone: The Collapse and Revival of American Comunity* (New York: Simon & Schuster Paperbacks, 2000), 252. Putnam reports on the percentage of adults who attended church weekly in 1997-1998. For 18-29 year olds, it was 25 percent; for 30-44 year olds, it was 32 percent; for 45-59 year olds, it was 37 percent; and for 60+ year olds, it was 47 percent.
2. Ibid., 75-76. Putnam explains that since World War II, the percentage of Protestants in the U.S. population has declined 3 to 4 percent per decade, which adds up to 25 percent. The fraction of the population that claimed to be Protestant fell by nearly one-fifth from 1970 to 2000. The loss has been most felt in mainline Protestant denominations.

3. Ibid., 73.
4. Hannah Arendt, *The Life of the Mind* (Orlando: Harcourt, Inc., 1978).
5. Ethan Watters, *Urban Tribes: Are Friends the New Family?* (New York: Bloomsbury, 2003), 161.
6. According to the 1999 Auburn study reported by Jackson Carroll, *God's Potters: Pastoral Leadership and the Shaping of Congregations* (Grand Rapids, MI: Wm. B. Eerdmans Publishing Co.), 71-72.
7. Carroll, *God's Potters*, 78.
8. Jackson Carroll, "The Clergy Shortage: What it Means for Churches," *Presbyterian Outlook*, October 2, 2006.
9. Bill Lancaster and Jerry L. Van Marter, "Way Ahead for 'Hard-to-call' Churches Outlined." Accessed on October 3, 2006.
10. Carroll, *God's Potters*, 164.
11. Ibid., 90.
12. Dean R. Hoge and Jacqueline E. Wenger, "Experiences of Protestant Ministers Who Left Local Church Ministry," presented to the Religious Research Association, Norfolk, VA, October 25, 2003.
13. Carroll, *God's Potters*, 173-174.
14. Tim Kershner, "UCC General Synod endorses support for seminarians," *Worldwide Faith News*, July 15, 2006.
15. Carroll, *God's Potters*, 225. According to Carroll's research, one-third of the ministers who were ordained in the last ten years still had outstanding educational debt. In 2004, the cost, on average, of educating a Master of Divinity student was $100,000 and a 1991 Auburn Seminary study found that 1991 graduates averaged over $11,000 of debts (a number that has no doubt increased). The Presbyterian Church (USA) website reported a 2005 student loan debt of $32,959 (accessed on September 12, 2006).
16. Carroll, *God's Potters*, 68.
17. The Advocacy Committee for Women's Concerns (ACWC), "Clergywomen's Experiences in Ministry: Realities and Challenges," (Louisville: Office of the General Assembly, 2002).
18. Neela Banerjee, "Clergywomen Find Hard Path to Bigger Pulpit," *New York Times*, August 26, 2006.

19. ACWC, "Clergywomen's Experiences," 22. The 212th General Assembly of the Presbyterian Church directed the ACWC "to look at the emerging issues related to clergy women serving in parish ministry." The survey was compiled in 2002 and comprised the responses of 3853 clergywomen.

Chapter 7: Nurturing Spiritual Community

1. A great deal of this insight came from discussions with Karen Blomberg, a pastor, spiritual coach, and co-creator of The Authenticity Series.
2. Parker Palmer, *A Hidden Wholeness: The Journey Toward an Undivided Life* (San Francisco: Jossey Bass, 2004), 54.

Chapter 8: Growing Life

1. Diana Butler Bass, *The Practicing Congregation: Imagining a New Old Church* (Herndon, VA: The Alban Institute, 2004), 13.
2. Elizabeth Warren and Amelia Warren Tyagi, *The Two Income Trap: Why Middle-Class Mothers & Fathers Are Going Broke* (New York: Basic Books, 2003).
3. Alan Cooperman, "Faiths Condemn Homosexuality," *Washington Post,* November 17, 2006.
4. Psalm 1.
5. Ethan Watters, *Urban Tribes: Are Friends the New Family?* (New York: Bloomsbury, 2003), 16–17.
6. Friedrich Schleiermacher, *The Christian Faith* (T&T Clark, 1999).

CPSIA information can be obtained at www.ICGtesting.com
Printed in the USA
LVOW041932081211

258429LV00001B/5/P